Dany m. Poché

D1622572

Reprinted with permission from the author
by GOSPA FOUNDATION, INC.
105 Aguirre Street
Legaspi Village
Makati, Metro Manila

LIVING OUR PRIESTHOOD TODAY

OTHER BOOKS BY FATHER M. BASIL PENNINGTON

LIVING OUR PRIESTHOOD TODAY

by
Rev. M. Basil Pennington, o.c.s.o.
and
Rev. Carl J. Arico

Our Sunday Visitor Publishing Division
Our Sunday Visitor, Inc.
Huntington, Indiana 46750

ACKNOWLEDGMENTS

The Scripture texts contained in this work are taken from the *Revised Standard Version, Catholic Edition,* © 1965 and 1966 by the Division of Christian Education of the National Council of the Churches of Christ in the U.S.A., all rights reserved, and from the *New American Bible,* © 1970 by the Confraternity of Christian Doctrine, Washington, D.C., used by permission, all rights reserved. Other sources from which material has been excerpted or has served as the basis for portions of this work include those in the select bibliography of this work. Special thanks go to the Costello Publishing Co., Inc., for the use of brief excerpts taken from *Vatican Council II: The Conciliar and Post Conciliar Documents,* © 1975 by Costello Publishing Co., Inc., and Rev. Austin Flannery, O.P., general editor. The authors are grateful to the copyright holders for the use of their materials. If any copyrighted materials have been inadvertently used in this book without proper credit being given, please notify Our Sunday Visitor in writing so that future printings of this work may be corrected accordingly.

To
Bishop Charles R. Mulrooney
A TRULY PRIESTLY MAN
and
Joseph Arico
A FATHER WHO TAUGHT
THE MEANING OF "FATHER"
† MAY 27, 1987

Contents

Introduction

"And you call yourself a priest!" How many of us have heard that statement, and perhaps more than once. We have perhaps said it to ourselves. It can be said in many ways. Too many of us will hear it most strongly as a cry of derision, or maybe of disillusionment or despair. But I hope we hear it also as a powerful affirmation — especially in those times of greater illumination, when perhaps just for a moment or two, we get some insight into what really happened to us when two episcopal hands rested on our heads and words were spoken — a moment of awe: *And you call yourself a priest.*

Yes, we are priests. And not just according to the order of Melchizedek, but according to the new order of the covenant of Jesus Christ, intimate partakers of his own priesthood. Certainly, every Christian shares in the priesthood of Jesus Christ. Our aim here is not so much to set us apart and show how we are different — though we are set apart and are different — but to explore together the fullness of who we are and what that means in practice.

I have long been asked to write a book on "priestly spirituality." I have hesitated for just as long and I am still hesitant. Readers, I think, tend to put too much authority in the printed word. I and my coauthor, Father Carl Arico, speak only with the authority of fellow Christians, fellow priests, fellow travelers, fellow human beings. We want to share some reflections on our common, and at times not so common, journey as priests among the pilgrim People of God.

I must confess the word "spirituality" puts me off. If

9

there is one expression I dislike, it is that of "spiritual life." We are not spirits. We are men of flesh and blood; we have a real life, very concrete, very incarnational. When people speak of a spirit, they usually think of something quite undefined, something belonging to another world, rather nebulous and puffy, something about which we can do little or nothing. This translates over to spiritual life: something quite nebulous, about which we can do little. Priests who are eminently practical, who can build and maintain multimillion-dollar plants and create and supervise programs for the multitudes, abandon every bit of their practicality and of their effectiveness when it comes to their spiritual life.

Another illusion that flows out of the use of this expression is that we act as though our spiritual life were only a part of our life. We compartmentalize and we equate our spiritual life with time set aside for "spiritual exercises" (building up our spiritual physique!); then the rest of the time we don't have to worry about being spiritual.

Our spiritual life is our *real* life. It is the only life we have. If spiritual life means for us our life in the Spirit, or our life as animated by the Holy Spirit — our whole life, all that we say and think and do — then I can accept the term spiritual life. But honestly, is that what it usually means to you when you speak of your spiritual life?

Spirituality tends to take on the same connotations as spiritual life. It is too often seen as being merely those things that pertain to the spiritual life. *Spirituality is, rather, a basic, habitual attitude, the way in which a person constantly acts and receives life in accord with his or her innermost self, that self which has been Christed and Christed in a particular way according to the individual's gifts and charisms.* Spirituality pertains to every aspect of life, to our whole journey, every step of the way.

In this book we will talk about many aspects of our lives as priests. All of them we share with all other Christians — if we understand celibacy in the larger context of being a way in which we live out the sexual dimension of our lives. But we are concerned here with these aspects precisely insofar as they are animated by who we are as men whose configuration to Christ has been modified by our priestly ordination. In our first chapter we will try to see more clearly just what this means. For now, let it be enough to insist that spirituality, far from being a compartment of our lives, is concerned with integrity, with consistency, with the wholeness of our lives — the whole of our lives as an appropriate expression of who we are as men who have been called to follow Christ into the mystery of the Trinity and have been ordained to serve as priests among the Christian people, within the living Body of Christ.

In speaking of the priesthood I am very keenly aware of my limitations. My own ministry has been unique (hasn't every priest's?) and quite limited. Most significantly, I have never served in a parish. I do identify deeply with all my brother priests in all their varied ministries. In my love for you and for your ministry, my brother priests, I think I can authentically speak of "our parishes," "our students," and so on. Love bonds — but it does not necessarily make up for lived experience.

I recall an incident that took place some years ago. I had been invited to speak to the priests of my native diocese. In the question period that followed my talk, the first intervention came from a priest with whom I had been in the seminary. In substance he expressed his feeling that I was trying to force upon parish priests a spirituality that belongs to the monk. While I do not think that was the case, I understand well the feeling. It can be challenging when an "outsider" looks in and speaks candidly about what he sees. True, the outsider may be missing quite a bit, even some key aspects. But if we listen, we can learn. We can extract what is helpful. It is not good to block out the challenge. An outsider does see things differently and that has value. I do speak out of over twenty-five years of listening to priests, who have humbled me by their humility and openness. In some respects mine has been a privileged position. Priests sensing a place of special grace, a place apart, have opened wide their hearts in the silence of the monastic retreat.

Nonetheless, once I had accepted the responsibility to write this book, I began consulting every priest I could. In the course of that consultation I approached Father Carl. Having had a very broad experience in the course of his twenty-seven years in the priesthood — besides his parish work and ministry to diocesan priests, he has led workshops and retreats for priests in over seventy dioceses — Carl not only had a lot to offer, he wanted to contribute wholeheartedly to the preparation of this volume. He felt strongly that diocesan priests should contribute to the discussion of priestly spirituality. We soon began to think in terms of coauthorship, feeling that our very diverse lived experiences of the priesthood would complement each other and produce a richer and more complete reflection on the priestly journey. Not only did Carl and I share this desire to reflect together on our diverse journeys, we also had a special bond in our commitment to contemplative prayer. We have both been working to help our Church refind its contemplative dimension through Centering Prayer, supporting the work of the Contemplative Outreach Program.

You might be interested in how we proceeded with our task. After some months of reflection, we had our first work meeting. We sought to find a title that would speak to those to whom we wanted to speak, and catch the feeling of the approach we wanted to take. (The title was subsequently changed by the publisher.) We then made a collection of the topics that had surfaced in the course of our reflections during the previous months and in our conversations with other priests and lay persons, and we sought to bring these together into some order. When we had decided in a general way on the contents of the ten chapters, we divided them between ourselves according to our dominant interests and experience. Each of us then put on tape all the thoughts we had in regard to the chapters the other was going to draft and we exchanged these tapes. We were now ready to write our respective chapters. The drafts were sent back and forth. Finally, we spent a week together, bringing our common endeavor to completeness. Each chapter, then, is basically the work of one of us carrying the reflections of both of us — and greatly enriched by the contributions of many others: great theologians like Rahner, popular writers like Bernanos, priests who have shared their experience in writing like McGinnity (a bibliography at the end of the volume will try to acknowledge these published contributors), and many, many other priests and lay persons. To each we owe a debt of gratitude, and we trust they will find some reward in seeing produced — thanks to their contribution — a better volume in service of their brother priests.

Some may find the two of us rather conservative in our reflections. I do hope we are truly conserving all that is best in our living tradition. Others may find some of our thinking a bit far-out. We have been trying to listen with very open ears as well as very open hearts and minds. Still some will find our reflections and considerations are not actual enough — too taken up with the practical concerns of middle America, trying to ground these in a deeper thinking, but virtually prescinding from the greater questions of our times: a world shaken on its foundations by the violent, inhuman events of our century, challenged by the new world views being promulgated by physics, new computer mathematics, and other scientific disciplines. Perhaps one of the reasons we priests are not as alive, relevant, and effective as we might be is because we are not sufficiently in touch with these lessons. Maybe we need to ask ourselves, "Are these realities impacting on the lives of our people at deeper levels than we are usually addressing or ministering to? Does a prevailing constrictedness or superficiality in our sense of humanity result in a ministry that is not touching the deeper fears and pain that our people can hardly articulate but constantly live with?"

There are those — and I don't think they are in the

minority, at least among the younger clergy and laity —
who believe that there needs to be a radical rethinking
and restructuring in the life and ministry of priests in
general and of diocesan priests in particular, and anything less is putting Band-Aids on an open and gaping
wound. To some extent I am inclined to agree with these
men and women. Yet, if one is really wounded, he needs
some bandaging if he is to survive; the person who is hun-
gering needs some nourishment if he is going to be
around to enjoy the renewed priestly life later and, indeed, to take a part in bringing it into being. I hope what
we offer here will prove to be some nourishing food to
strengthen and encourage today's priests so that we can
courageously and unflaggingly undertake the immense
task of radical renewal in thought and in life. The priest
who cries for a radical renewal and restructuring, but
does not see himself as a part of bringing it about, and at
great personal cost, is kidding himself. Our heavenly Father profoundly respects the freedom and power he has
given us. If we want renewal, it will come about only by
our efforts — efforts that are wholly energized by his
grace. Renewal will not be handed to us on a platter. It
will be brought about by great effort that melts down the
old and patiently reshapes it. The work must essentially
be initiated in each one of us. Yet we cannot be satisfied
with reforming ourselves. An essential part of our own
reformation is an effective realization that the key to any
renewal of the priesthood is a deep sense of our interconnectedness, a caring because we are one — no one grows
or is renewed without the other. Diocesan and religious
priests need to sense deeply this interconnectedness and
it needs to be experienced by our people. We are all the
People of God, the Church, the Body — and each member, each cell, affects and is affected by each other, by
each cell-member. We are all children of the world,
meant to be leaven — certainly a source of compassionate caring and sharing.

Albert Einstein is quoted as saying that with the ar-
rival of the atomic age everything was changed except

14

our thinking. We might also say that with the coming of Pope John XXIII and the Second Vatican Council everything was changed except our thinking. It is most difficult to be fully renewed in thought. It is only by plunging into the Source of all that we can come out wholly transformed by that transforming Spirit who has been blowing so mightily upon us during these last twenty years of journeying. We will be talking more about this "plunging into the Source" in the course of these pages. Carl and I have been seeking to do this as fully and as faithfully as we can in the course of our work. But we are profoundly aware that there is so much more yet to be seen and understood, not to speak of its being expressed in our lives and in our words.

In our writing — and the unity of the book lies in this — we have constantly sought to make sense of our lives as priests as we have come to understand the priesthood in these post-Vatican II days. The sum proves to be a rather untidy package with parts bulging and popping out in many directions. No attempt has been made to smooth it all out. It reminds me of that interesting little church in Rome, Saint Georgio Valebro. It was built of all sorts of odds and ends. It creates an interesting place of worship, achieving a certain beauty and balance because of its simplicity and its focus on the sanctuary. It is a focus that, we hope, brings this book together. Unity is sought and found at the deeper level, an identification with Jesus Christ priest who came to minister. His own life and ministry did not quite all fit together, at least in the judgment of most around him: friends, family, and foes. Yet for him it had a unity, a single thrust, and ultimate meaning: "I do always the things that please the Father." He and the Father are one — yet two. We and Christ are one — yet two. He succeeded in doing always the things that please the Father. We often fail in doing always the things that please him — though perhaps not as often as we tend to fault ourselves for — but we can at least make this our unifying goal: to do always the things that please our Lord. All that is part and parcel of our lives ultimately is confronted with this central concern: Is the Lord, who shares with me his priestly way of being, pleased to be with me in this?

Young people are sometimes disconcerting in the frank honesty of their expression. Our novices refer to the conferences given to them by the novice master as "repetitions." Is there anything new under the sun? We have heard it all before. That fact can lead us to approach even the Gospels with a certain jadedness that prevents us from hearing them again with a certain freshness. We have heard it all before, but we will hear it differently now. Both hearer and speaker are in a different space; both have grown and changed, and so has the whole context within which we interact. We have heard it before, but we have never heard it as we will hear it now if we have the courage to drop filtering mind-sets and receive the word into our own actual present life experience. In this book we don't pretend to say anything new, but what we say comes out of new lived experiences, with new shadows and lights, with new Spirit — it is wholly new. May you enjoy it with a newness of mind and be refreshed (in the literal sense of that word: made fresh again in your priestly spirit) by it. May the Spirit, who has brought this alive within us, bring it alive within you according to your own unique reality as a priest of Jesus Christ.

As you read along we would like to suggest that you stop from time to time, at least at the end of each chapter. Rest a little. Be aware of the presence of the Holy Spirit. Get in touch with what is going on. How do you *feel* about what is being said? What do you *think* about it? If a close friend were with you right now, what would you want to say, to share? What questions are coming up for you? What is the Lord saying to you? What do you want to say to him? It is time for prayer — this is prayer.

And do pray for us. Thank you for allowing us to share our thoughts with you.

FATHER BASIL

Holy Thursday, 1987

1

Who Are We?

●

On the day we were ordained, we probably heard more than once: "You are a priest forever." A priest! What does that mean? How radically did the change that took place on the day of ordination affect our identity as human persons? Who are we priests?

What is our priestly identity? It is not as clear as it might seem. Recently I had the privilege of being on sabbatical for a year. During the course of the year I attended the Vatican II Institute for Clergy Education at Menlo Park, California. One of the presenters was Father Ken Osborne, O.F.M., who explored the topic of sacraments. He devoted a large portion of his time to the sacrament of holy orders. With great interest I listened to Ken as he outlined the historical background of our priesthood. I waited for his conclusion. As best I can recall, this is what he came to: a priest is one who can say, "I believe, I am a sacrament of the one priest, one teacher, one leader, Jesus Christ."

This was a powerful statement, and yet after I pondered over it, it did not satisfy me personally. Somehow I

17

knew that I needed more, something more definite. Both Basil and I struggled with this need and what I now share with you is what makes sense to me as a good foundation for my ongoing journey.

Each year on Holy Thursday, or some chosen day close to that day, we gather in the cathedral to celebrate our priesthood. This celebration is then carried back into our parishes and religious communities as all the People of God seek to experience together a renewed sense of the priesthood. It can be a challenging moment for us — we hear again those questions that were addressed to us in the cathedral on the day of our ordination: "Are you resolved, with the help of the Holy Spirit, to discharge without fail the office of priesthood in the rank of presbyters as the trusted partners of the bishops in caring for the Lord's flock? Are you resolved to celebrate the mysteries of Christ faithfully and religiously as the Church has handed them down for the glory of God and the sanctification of Christians? Are you resolved to exercise the ministry of the Word worthily and with wisdom, preaching the Gospel and explaining the Catholic faith? Are you resolved to unite yourself more closely every day to Christ, the first priest who offered himself for us to the Father as a perfect sacrifice, and to consecrate your life to God for the salvation of all?"

Because of our publicly expressed commitment to these resolutions we priests are called to be leaders in our daily search for holiness and our daily witness of fidelity. This is our vocation, this is our call, this is the way we profess and live our faith.

Because of the awesome dimensions of our call and profession, I would like to approach our identity as if it were a mosaic, looking at various pieces that will eventually create a total image. There is always a struggle between the ideal and the real, the dream and the reality. If we cling solely to an ideal and do not accept the real, we will fly about ineffectively. If we let go of the ideal and settle solely for what is here and now the real, our lives and ministry will have no forward thrust, nothing toward which to aim, no vision to call us forth. What we want to do is to keep the ideal fully alive and at the same time lovingly embrace the real and gently lead it toward the fullness of the ideal. While we are on our journey our identity lies in a combination of the two, a blending that is not without its tensions. These are life-giving, vitalizing tensions.

The way our particular journey has unfolded since our ordination has undoubtedly been deeply influenced by the year in which we were ordained, what has happened since then, and the sort of assignments we have received. Wherever we have been assigned, whatever the positions we have held, we have all had to deal with the evolving "myths" of the priesthood. I was ordained in the year 1960 and I have experienced a considerable shift in the ways in which our people and we ourselves have regarded our priestly identity. I can remember when most of our people were in awe of the priest. We were looked up to as some special breed of human being, made over by six years of seclusion; we were admired and honored, but not to be imitated, for we were "out of this world." I can remember conversations during which a person would suddenly stop and say, "Oh, I'm sorry, Father. I didn't mean to say that in front of you." We were not supposed to know about a lot of things. Our sacred ears were not to be violated by worldly talk. We were automatically supposed to be community leaders, men of wisdom who had the answers. We were, in great part, "mystery men." We were the ministers of the *mystery* of Christ in his sacramental presence and life.

For those ordained after the directives of the Second Vatican Council began to take effect, the initial scenario would have been different. Seminary training still inculcated an image of priesthood and drew the ideal picture, but that image and ideal, even in the latter days of seminary training, was confronted with the real. More and more a priest has had to face an image that has been created by the people. In many places, attentiveness to us as priests is no longer something automatic. Our better-educated parishioners wait to see if we are really worthy of their respect, if we do really have leadership qualities, if we are all we are supposed to be.

Certainly, the situation differs from one area to the other, even within our own country. From my own experience — that of leading workshops and retreats in all parts of the nation — I have come to believe that the fifty states are fifty states of mind, which break down even more within each state. In some areas much of the mystery of the priesthood still survives. More generally in suburbia and the newer neighborhoods I find the priesthood not regarded as so mysterious, but rather looked upon more in a professional way: the priest is a man who has a profession.

A lot could be said about greatly differing individual situations. What is evident is that, for better or worse, profound and far-reaching changes have taken place.

The aura of mystery may be gone or greatly diminished, yet the mystery itself will always be there. It is within each one of us as priests. And this, perhaps, is what is more significant: the shift that has taken place within us. While before, the people were awed by the mystery of our priesthood, we ourselves tended to see everything as clear and orderly, with the clear distinctions of a well worked-out scholastic theology. Now, when things seem clearer or more comprehensible to the people — they now know what they expect of us — we have become more aware of the mystery of Christ's presence in us, the mystery of being priests.

I stand in awe of the depths of love that Christ has for me. The Curé of Ars says it beautifully: "Oh, the priest is something great; if he knew it all, he would die." I stand in awe of the interior journey that I am being called to. I stand in awe of the depths of the love within the people that I journey with, in awe of their love for me as a man, Christian, and priest. I stand in awe of the Church in the profoundness of its Christ-presence in the world — the Church, with all its strengths and weaknesses, still being a presence of Christ in this world here and now.

Someone has turned the tables. The myth has become enfleshed and is touching our daily lives. We have a number of choices on how we can respond to this change. We can refuse to allow the change to happen in our lives and try to hold on to the grand myth of old: the priest on his pedestal and the people below. We can let the myth go entirely and at the same time let go of the mystery of priesthood, reducing our role to something purely functionary, one among the many services found in our society. Or we can accept the myth, insofar as it still exists, and the mystery and the reality, and live with the healthy tensions that come from this. By myth I mean the projected image that people have of us. The mystery is the actual presence of Christ within us working through the priesthood, and the reality is what we know to be in the depths of our hearts in regard to the myth and the mystery within us.

This growth-producing tension can express itself in different ways and in various degrees.

We experience it in the assaults on the image of the priest in the mass media. In such a climate we can feel vulnerable, experience some doubt, some loss of nerve, timidity, and even perhaps an inability to encourage others to become priests. This causes us, not only to feel bad about ourselves, but even about the priesthood in general. Whether it's watching a talk show on television or reading a review of a book or even going to the movies, all too often the troubles and insecurities that people experience seem to be centered on the Church and on the priest.

We are also assaulted by individuals. When we are invited to social gatherings, a good number of times we find people approaching us to debate current issues: the Church's stand on racism, abortion, family life and human sexuality, the role of women, celibacy and married priests, the closing of Catholic schools, clericalism, and so on. There we are, perhaps with a drink in hand, at the end of a weary day, being drawn into the debate of the century. And somewhere, in the middle of it all, we find that we, the priestly fraternity, are to blame for all the ills of the world. To make matters even more difficult, in these exchanges we sometimes find ourselves seriously questioning the position of the magisterium, which we are asked to defend (not so much regarding the principles involved, but regarding the application of the principles to the individual situation). One bishop recently commented about the present atmosphere in this way, "I just go about my business as usual, but I must admit I am starting to look over my shoulder every once in a while."

In spite of all this I would not like to go back to the old situation where there was no communication or no dialogue in regard to the sensitive issues of our times. What we are experiencing flows from a climate of openness that has been created since Vatican II. Our people have been freed from some of their inhibitions. If we are willing to listen, and if our people sense that they will be heard, then they will feel free to let us know what they believe and feel, and sometimes in no uncertain terms. It seems to be part of our American way to speak out when there is the freedom to do so.

Sometimes the expectations directed toward us as priests can be overwhelming. I remember attending a parish council meeting with one of our regional bishops in order to hear the expectations of the council in regard to a new pastor. The council members presented us with a printed copy of their expectations: A priest who cares deeply about his vocation, who is willing to be available and present to the needs of our people, who is willing to use others' gifts and talents, especially those of our deacon, our DRE, our youth minister, and our committees; one of broad scope and vision; one who is knowledgeable in theology and ecclesiology; who is emotionally stable and who can deal with criticism in a constructive manner and who has strong appreciation of and respect for other Christian denominations without in any way compromising those beliefs and practices that are uniquely Catholic.

I recall our surprise and the bishop's response: "I know only two people that can fulfill this job description:

myself and Jesus, and I'm not too sure about Jesus." This became a stock reply at many a future council meeting when expectations and hopes and dreams were presented, but presented in such a way that they had to be fulfilled by one man. For those in other ministerial situations, the expectations are also often piled up, especially for religious priests: the job is to be done professionally, the proper degrees obtained, the image of the religious community maintained in this particular place, a traditional style is to be observed, and at the same time the priest is to be faithful to all his commitments within the community. Within the community there are not only the local meetings but the larger meetings concerned with the renewal and implementation of rules and constitutions, possibly a call to support the mission activities of the community, and always a responsibility to go along with the decisions affecting the overall well-being of the congregation.

Demands made upon us in our rectories or religious houses can be unreasonable and even demeaning. I recall one story concerning a fifty-year-old priest, assigned as a parochial vicar to a parish after many years of social-action ministry. At dinner he was informed by the pastor: "One of your duties here will be to take down the flag every night." The priest replied, "I am fifty years old, too old for the Cub Scouts. Let them take it down." A long discussion ensued. The priest concluded: "If I ever live with someone again, it won't be a man." In rectories and religious houses there are legitimate demands made on us for the sake of community: prayer in common, meetings, and the different responsibilities that must be taken care of within the house. But once the priest has fulfilled his share of the communal effort he should be left free to use his time as he sees best. I remember a situation where a priest was popular as a workshop leader. When he had fulfilled his community obligations, he would go to present workshops in the neighboring parishes. He met with some resistance within the house because he was expending his labors elsewhere.

Further expectations can be directed toward us from those on the diocesan or provincial level. In one diocese there was a task force set up by the priests' senate to enhance the skills of priests as pastoral leaders. The task force decided the priests should have an attitude that would allow them to be able to cope with change; to be open to a Vatican II model of Church; to have flexibility and adaptability; to be psychologically independent; to be open to the attitude of others; to possess verbal and nonverbal communication skills as well as listening ability; to demonstrate assertiveness and knowledge of the process of confrontation; to be familiar with techniques for organization and management, planning and goal setting, problem solving and decision making; and to be a collegial, relational, human, pastoral, and community-building person. In the ideal order, of course, we would all like to have all of these skills, and they are to some extent necessary to carry out our mission with total success. In reality, it is almost impossible for someone to have all of these skills.

In our expectations, we overload and overwhelm each other in an attempt to renew and challenge one another to growth. In addition, there are the expectations we place on ourselves. This we do in many ways. We like to achieve. We like to make progress. We need to be creative and competitive. This might not be so bad if we can learn with a spirit of compassion to direct the compulsiveness of our activity in order to rise to real new life. The trap lies in measuring ourselves and our priesthood by the number of people affected, the program initiated, the responsibilities fulfilled, the degrees attained, the title gained, and the projects completed. Bigger is better!

In spite of all of this, the priest stands where he has always stood, "in the middle," the mediator between God and creation, with the institutional Church behind him and the people before him, accountable to both. I have worked with many priests and am amazed that with all the expectations and with the climate as it is today, with all that is going on, we still are able to function. We still are able to be present to our ministry, to be present to our people. We still are able to do what needs to be done. How many times I have seen situations where the professionals — the psychologists, the doctors, the police, the corporate leaders — have given up on people. They've expressed the belief that there's nothing more that can be done. Then the priest has come in and has been able to salvage more than anyone thought possible. In some cases he has quite literally brought people back to life. How we can best go about such ministry with friendship and prayer and discernment we will consider in the following chapters. We tend to spend enough time on the *how* of the priesthood. No vocation can be defined solely by functions. Let us now look into the *what* of the priesthood.

I've heard many priests ask: "What is a priest? What is the role of the priest today? What is his special identity in the community of believers?" With the renewal we have seen a new emphasis on shared responsibility. Today, competent lay persons and permanent deacons perform many of the functions formerly reserved to priests. Theologians as well as Church practice seem to be amplifying the role of the laity while diminishing the significance of the ministry of the ordained priests. As one priest put it, he feels like one of the Three Musketeers, staving off hordes who are trying to remove him from the altar. A little humor never hurts. In fact, it can help us to get through some heavy stuff.

When we speak of priesthood, we speak of one priesthood, the priesthood of Jesus Christ. Jesus is the sole mediator; we participate in this priesthood. There is the priesthood of all believers, which is shared by all the baptized, ordained and nonordained. "You are a chosen race, a royal priesthood, a holy nation, God's own people, that you may declare the wonderful deeds of him who called you out of darkness into his marvelous light" (1 Peter 2:9). Vatican II's *Dogmatic Constitution on the Church* affirms the common priesthood of all the faithful. Through baptism each Christian is consecrated by the Spirit and possesses the characteristics of a priest. The document then goes on to state that there is a distinction between the priesthood of all believers and the ordained, or ministerial, priesthood. The Latin text uses two words, *sacerdos* and *presbyter*. Every baptized person is a *sacerdos*, but not everyone is a *presbyter*. Through the sacrament of holy orders one becomes a *presbyter* and is given a new function in the community of *sacerdotium*. As Vatican Council II tells us: "Though they differ essentially and not only in degree, the common priesthood of the faithful and the ministerial or hierarchical priesthood are none the less ordered one to another; each in its own proper way shares in the one priesthood of Christ" (*Dogmatic Constitution on the Church*, No. 10).

The ministerial priesthood complements the priesthood of all believers. The bishop enjoys the fullness of the ministerial priesthood. The presbyters and deacons participate with him in the sacrament of holy orders in different degrees. Together they create a sacrament of unity.

Having stated the general picture, let us now explore a little more closely some of the details, keeping them always in the total context. Let us also tap into our living tradition to see what it offers us to complete the picture of our identity as men ordained into the Church's ministerial priesthood.

The story of salvation is a story of God's communication with his people in a human manner. God totally respects our human condition. With us he operates in space and time. In this operation God chose a moment in human history and a place in our world to send his only begotten Son into our family to bring grace and mercy to us in human words and gestures.

Christ himself is a sacrament. Jesus appeared and acted as any other man. His divine power was hidden and yet shown through his human condition. In Jesus, God truly "pitched his tent among us." He walked this earth on his Father's behalf to teach and rule and sanctify the

People of God. He did not do this as an angel; he did it as a human being, an embodied spirit.

But what about now? Jesus is no longer visibly present. How are we to come in contact with God? The visible "Body of the Lord" in space and time now is the Church, the sign and reality of salvation, the sacrament of Christ's presence. In the theology of the Church as sacrament there are two central truths: the Church is Christ, present and active; and the Church is Christ, visible in the world.

As Christ walked the earth he ministered, taught, and sanctified. So the Church today as a visible reality ministers, teaches, and sanctifies. Pius XII expressed this beautifully in 1945 in his encyclical on the Mystical Body. It is expressed even more profoundly in Vatican II's *Dogmatic Constitution on the Church*. Both deserve rereading and reflection. One example from Vatican II: Christ "continually provides in his body, that is, in the Church, for gifts of ministries through which, by his power, we serve each other unto salvation so that, carrying out the truth in love, we may through all things grow unto him who is our head" (*Dogmatic Constitution on the Church*, No. 7).

What then does Christ present in his Church do? He draws us through the historical visibility of his Church into visible communion with himself and with one another. As the *Dogmatic Constitution on the Church* expresses it: God "has, however, willed to make" human persons "holy and save them, not as individuals without any bond or link between them, but rather to make them into a people who might acknowledge him and serve him in holiness . . . It is Christ indeed who has purchased it [the Church] with his own blood. . . ; he has filled it with his Spirit; he has provided means adapted to its visible and social union. All those, who in faith look towards Jesus, the author of salvation and the principle of unity and peace, God has gathered together and established as the Church, that it may be for each and everyone the visible sacrament of their saving unity" (No. 9).

The primary way that the Church has for drawing us is its very nature as a visible community of love and faith. In being drawn to the Church we are being drawn to Christ. And in this drawing we become involved in a network, an embodiment of the message of Christ's love and faith.

All of the Council's documents emphasize this embodied unity. For me Father William Dodd summarizes this teaching well: "The Church is the sacrament of saving unity. The Church is the sign and reality of the risen Lord, the savior of all, the head of the universe. Among those who are his visible members Christ actively works in word and sacrament for an ever deeper communion of love and faith. But through those who are his visible members through the community of love and faith which is the sign and reality of his salvation, Christ the head actively works to draw all humankind to visible communion with himself. In summary: the Church is the sacrament, the sign and reality of this salvific community-forming activity of Christ."

In the body of the Church there is both head and members. This must be visibly manifested in the Church and this is the sacramental significance of the hierarchy and the faithful in the Church.

The hierarchy are the sacrament of Christ the Head; the faithful are the sacrament of Christ the members. "A difference in kind, not just degree." It is important to remember that the hierarchy are members of the believing Church just as the faithful, and that the faithful share by collaboration in the ministry of the hierarchy, though a real distinction remains. This is brought out in the *Decree on the Ministry and Life of Priests*: "Through that sacrament priests by the anointing of the Holy Spirit are signed with a special character and so are configured to Christ the priest in such a way that they are able to act in the person of Christ the head" (No. 2).

This special character that we receive in the sacrament of holy orders creates an ontological effect in us. Various authors speak not only of a configuration but also use terms such as "made over," "an embodiment" of Christ the Head, the head forming community.

Our identity as priests only makes sense when it is rooted in Christ and in the Church. This calls for a renewal of our faith, our faith in Christ, and our faith in the Church. Our faith in Christ needs to grow to such an extent that our goal in life becomes more and more visible as being a living-out of that supreme prayer: "through him, with him, and in him, in union with the Holy Spirit, all glory and honor is yours, Almighty Father, for ever and ever." Our faith in the Church needs to embrace not only the local community of believers and not only the mystical Church as the sacrament of saving unity but also the larger institutional Church, the structure that has been called forth by Christ to allow his Church, as a visible reality, to continue through the ages. There needs to be in us a renewal of faith in this reality. For if our faith in the saving power of Christ and the saving unity of the Church is weak, then our priesthood, in a real sense, is cut off from its main source of power and life. No matter what are the expectations of the people, of our community, of those in authority, and even of ourselves, the essence of our priesthood is acting in the person of Christ the head, Christ forming a community of love and faith. In the context of the Church, we are sacraments of unity. That is what the priest is.

Pope John Paul II in October, 1986, when giving a retreat to priests at Ars, expressed concern that the identity of the priest was being placed solely within the context of his functions. He affirmed that we are more than our role and more than our functions. And then he went on to say: "This is so, first of all, because we are marked in our very soul through ordination with a special character which configures us to Christ the priest so that we are made capable of acting personally in the name of Christ the Head. Certainly, it is true that we are taken from among the people and that we remain close to them, 'Christians with them,' as Saint Augustine said. But we are 'set apart,' totally consecrated to the work of salvation: 'The function of the priest in that it is united in the episcopal order shares in the authority with which Christ himself builds up, sanctifies and governs his body.' It is the Second Vatican Council that recalls this to us."

Some may wonder: If we can clearly establish this as our identity as priests, whether diocesan or religious, then will we have uniformity in the way priesthood is expressed and lived out? My answer to that is: No. We will not, because although the priesthood is one, we still live out our priesthood according to our own gifts and charisms and historical conditioning. There will always be diversity in expression.

At the first convocation (1981) of priests in the archdiocese of Newark, this tension between uniformity and diversity was tested. There we were, over six hundred priests of all ages, together for four days, free from our usual responsibilities. Many had mixed reactions as to the value of the gathering. The keynote speaker was Father Walter Burghardt. He suggested to us that as our model of Church so our model of priesthood. I would like to share with you how he developed the models of Church of Avery Dulles.

If our model of Church is *institutional*, then we will see hierarchical structure and organization as primary and our model of priesthood will be institutional and hierarchical. We will tend to lean in that direction, to be highly organized and see clearly our role as the leader: the priest is leader. With this model the expected response is that all know their role and express their loyalty to the general structure.

If our model of Church is *community/communion*, then our model of priesthood will be that of builder of community. We will want to explore all the elements that are essential for a community of love and of faith. We will devote time to process and procedure to make sure people have a real sense of ownership. The expected response here is that all know that participation and shared responsibility are essential.

If our model of Church is that of *sacrament*, then

our model of priesthood will be one of sacramental ministry. The sacramental, liturgical life will be the essential element of our priesthood. There will be much study, reflection, and planning. We will see ourselves as those presiding over the worshiping community. The response we will expect from those to whom we minister will be full and active participation in the liturgy.

If the model of the Church that we embrace is that of *herald*, then our model of priesthood will be that of the proclaimer of the word of God. Study, meditation, and the preaching of the word will occupy our time and attention. This will have priority among our services. We will offer our people every opportunity to share in conversation, expecting in them a change of heart, a conversion.

If our model of Church is that of *servant*, then our model of priesthood will also be one of servant: to be available to the people, to be present to them. Our presence will extend to the needs of the world, the questions of social justice, and the need to reach out and to respond. The response of those around us will be measured by their availability to others, and by their awareness and commitment to the social issues of the time: By their fruits you shall know them.

Father Burghardt found the common unifying bond of all the models is *discipleship*. This is the ultimate model of all ministry — to be a disciple. We will see the Church as responding to the promptings of the Holy Spirit, of having a good self-knowledge, an ability to accept itself as it is and the willingness to be open. These will be reflected in our own lives. Thus we will be ever on the spiritual journey to a deeper realization of the presence of the Lord in our lives. We will cultivate a willingness to follow the Spirit wherever he may lead us and this will be what we will expect from those with whom we minister.

With some reflection each of us will perceive what model of the Church is our primary preference, a preference that is effective on so many different levels. It may be a reasoned conclusion or just an intuition, but it is there. We are aware of it when we come in contact with those who hold another model as their primary preference. The question is: Can we make room for diverse models of Church? Can we make room for diverse models of priesthood? We have to, because the mystery of Church and priesthood is not defined by any one of these models. Its complete reality is the sum total of all the models. Remember the story of the three blind men who describe their experience of an elephant? One reported that the elephant was skinny and serpentine, for he came into contact with the tail; another reported that the elephant was like a large tree, for his contact was with the leg; the third said that the elephant was soft and flexible, for his contact was with the trunk. Were any of these wrong? No. Did any of them have the whole truth? No. But, by putting their experiences together, they were able to grasp more of the truth than any one of them had on his own.

That is the challenge to us in our quest for our priestly identity — to realize that together we can arrive at a fuller and more clear picture of the Church and of our priesthood. For example, can a priest who sees the Church and his priesthood primarily as institutional be open to the ideas and vision of the priest who sees the Church and priesthood as primarily community, and vice versa? This might demand of us a conversion, an opening of mind and heart, and on two levels — not just on the level of theory or model but also on the personal level. On the level of model, doesn't it make sense for us to be open to hear the wisdom and experience of those who know another model of Church and priesthood? If I am trying to live the servant model, reaching out and being available, sensitive to the needs of the believing community and of the world, isn't there something I can gain by amplifying my experience, reaching out and drawing upon the wisdom and experience of my brothers who are trying to live the other models? Would this not broaden my horizon and save me from any myopic view of Church and priesthood? Let us try to be open to the values to be found in other views of the mystery of Church and the mystery of priesthood. It is not a question of giving up or no longer believing in the model that we have been following, that we are drawn to, that we are most comfortable with; rather it is a question of building on it and enhancing it and knowing that there is room for growth without sacrificing what we already have.

It is part of our human condition that the degree to which we like or dislike the model lived by another we tend to like or dislike that person. We can all catalog the comments we have heard priests make describing one another: the institutional men with their ambitious loyalty, community men with their endless programs, sacramental men with their vestments and incense, heralds with Bibles and prayer groups, servants with their latest petition to be signed, and disciples with their witness stories. Thank God, there is a marvelous sense of humor among us. At the same time I ask God's forgiveness for the tendency to believe that I have all the answers. In today's situation, we can ill afford to be polarized, even by healthy differences of opinion and points of view. We need the support and affirmation of one another.

At our diocesan convocation all the models of Church and priesthood were present. We were all challenged to let go of our myopic tendencies, to look to one another, to learn and to grow. In the end Father Burghardt received a standing ovation. As the convocation proceeded, communication grew and grew. At the conclusion of our four days together we concelebrated the Eucharist, bishops and priests all together. We walked two by two to the altar to break bread together. It was a powerful manifestation of our priesthood as a sign of unity, forming community and celebrating it in the Eucharist. This was the high point of the convocation and a powerful witness to our call. The Christian priesthood has never been frozen in one model; it continues to develop and adapt itself in response to human situations. Each of us has received the gift of priesthood personally. We are called to develop an ever deeper Christian consciousness. We have a responsibility to keep growing in the realities of priesthood as they gradually unfold within us, around us, and among us. Our lives are grounded in the reality of life; our call to holiness as priests is grounded not in an out-of-the-world experience, but very much in an in-the-world experience, whether we are religious or diocesan, monks or social activists.

We are more than just men who have received a juridical commission from our bishop or superior. We are sacraments. We are what we are, not because of what we do but because of what we are. We are Christ the Head made visible in this place and time for the purpose of drawing humankind to community with Christ to the glory of the Father in union with the Holy Spirit. This is the ontological aspect that makes our priesthood differ from the priesthood of all the faithful. As Vatican Council II stated, it is a difference in kind, not just degree. I don't want to be misunderstood, but I do want to speak frankly to you. When we see ourselves solely as ministers of the Eucharist and absolution — as one author puts it, "sacrament confectors" and "word preachers" — we reduce our call to functions. No matter how sublime they may be, functions are still only functions. They do not give us an identity. It is true we do these things, but they have a meaningful existence only within the historical visibility of the Body of the risen Lord. They are sacramental actions of Christ the Head within his community of love and faith. We his priests are sacraments, acting in the person of Christ the Head. We are, before all else, Christ forming community in historical visibility. In the context of the Church, we are sacraments of unity. Here we live our spiritual journey. It is precisely in the forming of community that we deepen our personal and sacramental relationship with Christ the Head, and are transformed by Christ into Christ and grow in oneness with the larger community.

There has been discussion and misunderstanding as to what precisely is priestly work and what is not priestly work. There are those who believe that our priestly work lies primarily in the "cultic" aspects of our vocation.

Others maintain that priests as well as lay persons can minister in other fields, such as science, politics, and education. I recall a meeting with Archbishop Peter L. Gerety, during which one of the priests complained about priests being in what was called "special work," work outside the parish context. The archbishop replied, "As long as the work serves the diocese in its mission to the People of God, it is priestly work." The same question arises within religious communities. A priest-author is seen as being withdrawn from direct participation in the community's apostolate even though he is giving witness to the charism of his community through his writings.

It isn't really a question of priestly versus nonpriestly work; rather it is a question of where the Church needs to have the visibility of Christ-the-Head-forming-community present. When a priest-teacher is moved from a secular campus to a parish, it does not mean that he has moved from nonpriestly work to priestly work. There is simply a pastoral judgment being made that the needs of the Church are better served at this time by having this priest in this place.

Our spirituality as priests has to express itself not only in personal prayer and sacrifices, nor only in the cultic aspects of our ministry. It must also be lived out in our priestly work. And our priestly work is that work to which we have been assigned by the Church, as well as any other work we have been able to undertake, in order to give witness to Christ the Head, present, forming community. True priestly spirituality is a mediator spirituality. It demands a mystic of belonging both to God and to our fellow humans, bringing all visibly together. There is a paradox here because, in fact, we are already all one — one in God's creative love and more immediately one in Christ's redeeming grace. Our mission is to bring this invisible reality to a powerful, supportive, experiential visibility. It is in being catalysts of Christ-community that we are who we are and that we become holy. This is our proper identity. And true spirituality lies in living to the full who we truly are in Christ.

2

Charism
in Context

We have identified priesthood as the sacrament of Christ the Head, forming community within the mystery of the Church, the sacrament of saving unity. I would now like to explore more fully the context within which we live out our priesthood.

As a diocesan priest I am very conscious of the fact that some of the faithful compare us with religious priests and find us wanting. I remember an incident that took place in New York City some years ago. I was leading a three-day workshop on Centering Prayer. On the final night a woman came up to me and said, "You Jesuits are a real credit to the Church, with your training and your intelligence, not like my parish priest." When I told her I was not a Jesuit but a diocesan priest she thought I was kidding.

We also tend to put ourselves down. Perhaps you remember that scene from *The Great Impostor*. The local pastor is trying to help the overly idealistic youth who would develop into the great impostor. "Sometimes we have to accept second best. When I was young, I wanted to be a Trappist, the hardest, toughest, most holy in the Church. I went to a monastery, but after two years I had to leave. So I am a parish priest. It's something good. We do some good." I suspect at the time the film was first presented, most diocesan priests would have heard Father without flinching. Today, more aware of the universal call to holiness and the dignity of every Christian (indeed, of every person) and every Christian vocation, thanks to Vatican II, not as many of us would go along with this. Yet I wonder: How many of us really believe we parish priests have the same call to holiness as do our Trappist brothers? There are no second-class citizens nor second-class vocations within the Body of Christ.

In actual fact, some of the faithful feel we parish priests are closer to them and better able to help them. Recently a young man came to see me at the rectory to discuss his personal problems. He was not from the parish. When I asked why he had come to our parish, he replied, "What do the monks in my parish know about life? You guys are right out there with us."

People do have different expectations in regard to diocesan priests and religious priests because they perceive differences in the way we live. We priests all share essentially the same priesthood and have the same call to holiness. And yet we do live our priesthood in different ways. The differences express our respective charisms.

What do I mean by charism? The word comes from a Greek word meaning "a favor, an expression of kindness or a gift, a special manifestation of divine presence." It is an ability and an inclination to be of service in particular ways according to the gift that God has given us. John Futrell, in an excellent article that appeared in *The Way*, wrote of the charism of religious: "Discovering the founder's charism is simply a graced way of seeing and of following Jesus for the service of the Church. It can cease to exist if and when this particular vision and this service ceases to be a true good for the Church."

Can we also speak of charism in regard to the diocesan priest? Is there a special service, attitude, and approach that diocesan priests, in virtue of the grace of their vocation, bring to their ministry as priests? What is the special service, vision, and approach that religious priests of particular communities bring to their ministry precisely as religious priests? What is the special way that all priests mirror the presence of Christ in service of the Body of Christ?

We know that the Spirit is alive and operating in us and among us. The power of the Spirit that brought the Church to life on Pentecost is alive now in our lived situation. And we know that this presence of God will be with us till the end of time. There are three things that are very apparent when we examine closely the working of the Spirit within the Church. The first is that the Spirit is given to all. The second is that the Spirit empowers each of us to do something that is unique. And the third is that the Spirit brings about the continuing abiding of the presence of the Lord. What is that something unique that the Spirit empowers religious priests and diocesan priests to do? What is our empowerment? What is our special way of showing forth the abiding presence of the Lord in the Church through priesthood?

In general, our special role has been spelled out in the classical threefold ministry of teaching, leading, and sanctifying. Through ordination we have entered into a special relationship with Christ the Head in his teaching, priestly, and pastoral role.

John Paul II led a retreat for priests at Ars, a town whose renown depends wholly on the sanctity of a parish priest. In the course of the retreat he said:

> Indeed, what a wonderful thing it is to exercise our threefold priestly ministry as bishops or priests, a ministry that is indispensable to the Church:
>
> The ministry of one who proclaims the Good News: to make Jesus Christ known; to put men into a true relationship to him; to watch over the authenticity and fidelity of the faith, so that it may

neither be lacking nor changed or sclerotic; and also to keep alive in the Church the impulse of evangelization, and to form apostolic workers. The ministry of the one who dispenses the mysteries of God: to make them present in an authentic manner, especially to make present the paschal mystery by means of the Eucharist and of forgiveness of sin; to permit the baptized to have access to these, and to prepare them for this. The laity will never be able to be delegated to such ministries; a priestly ordination which permits one to act in the name of Christ the Head is necessary. The ministry, finally, of the pastor: to build up and maintain the communion among Christians, in the community which is entrusted to us, with the other diocesan communities, all linked to the successor of Peter. Before any specialization in view of his personal competence and in accord with his bishop, the priest is in fact minister of communion: in a Christian community that often risks rupture or closing in upon itself, he insures both the gathering together of the family of God and its openness. His priesthood confers on him the power to lead the priestly people.

The Second Vatican Council called upon religious communities to enter into a process of rediscovery and clarification of their founder's charism. In many institutes an elaborate process was undertaken to bring this about. Unfortunately, diocesan priests were never invited to do this. As one priest put it, the only directions we got were to implement the decrees of the Council and encounter all the reactions of the people. For this reason I ask religious priests to give us diocesan priests a moment here to catch up. I would like to take some time now to explore the charism of the diocesan priest. I do this because, with the changing scene within the Church, much frustration is experienced by diocesan priests. They have not identified their charism. I will explore first the charism of the diocesan priest and then I will offer some reflections on the religious charism. The reason

I proceed in this way is not to separate or divide us; it is simply a recognition that communication, cooperation, and collaboration are made possible when the giftedness of the various members is evident and understood.

What is the charism of the diocesan priest, the special way that we serve, manifesting the continuing event of the abiding presence of the Lord within the Body? I have conducted a number of retreats and workshops on this subject. In the process I have asked priests what they themselves think. Here are some of their responses: to be where the action is — coping with diversity with a spirit of acceptance — an enabler — a facilitator of the gifts of the laity — sharing the traditional work of the priest — the definer of vision for the community so that there might be a spirit of unity and peace — public relations people — living hospitality — a sense of presence with people seven days a week — a loving challenger — one who gives witness to the faith journey — the celebrator of life and liturgy — a local leader in the parish or in the diocese identified with the bishop. In further discussion some key concepts began to appear, concepts such as diocese, parish, individualism, unique style, authenticity, and the secular. I have come to see the charism of the diocesan priest as including six basic elements.

The first is *a special bonding with the bishop and the priests of the diocese.* This goes back to the earliest development of the priesthood within the Christian community and finds its roots in that historical reality.

Father Raymond Brown, in his *Priest and Bishop: Biblical Reflection,* explores first the Old Testament priesthood and then moves into the Christian priesthood of the first century. He emphasizes two things in regard to the Old Testament priests. First of all, they were intermediaries between God and their fellows; they were to proclaim to them God's will, teach them, and make sacrifices and other cultic offerings for them. Secondly, the priests formed a special priestly group. There was a strong interrelationship among them; they were the sons of Aaron.

At first, Christians remained very much a part of the Jewish community. But after the destruction of the temple (A.D. 70) three things took place: first, Christianity began to be separated from Judaism; second, the Eucharist was seen as an unbloody sacrifice — hence a priesthood was needed; and third, beginning with Clement of Rome, there was a call for a hierarchical structure similar to that in the Old Testament: a high priest with his assistant priests.

Jesus may not have historically established priesthood at the Last Supper. However, there was, at least, set in motion a process of forming followers to proclaim the kingdom, of developing community, and of establishing at the heart of those communities the passover meal as sacrifice, which postulated the need of a priestly leadership. During those first decades the bishop as successor of the Twelve was the one who was the primary proclaimer of the Good News and the leader at the celebration of the sacrificial meal. His assistants had more administrative roles to fulfill within the community.

Father James Mohler's book *The Origin and Evolution of the Priesthood* takes up, as it were, where Brown has left off and pushes on through the first four centuries of Christianity. During the second century, there was an increasing emphasis on the permanent residential community presided over by the bishop who was the chief administrator, judge, teacher, and presider at cultic celebrations. The presbyters were advisers to the bishop and lived with the bishop in the large cities. It was during the third century that presiding over the Eucharist was first delegated to priests in order that it might be celebrated in rural areas. Gradually, in the course of the fourth century, the priest was allowed to preside at the Eucharist and be the sign of unity in his own local community.

Historically, then, it is very clear that there is a special bonding between priest and bishop. This, of course, is still strongly expressed in the ordination ritual. They share in one priesthood, with their different roles. There is a bonding sacramentally, which is also hierarchical. The charism of the diocesan priest is very much connected with that of the bishop.

Besides this relationship with the bishop, history also gives witness to a special fraternity among the priests of the diocese. It is not surprising to see a strong response to the Emmaus Program and the Ministry to Priest Program of the Center for Human Development. These programs are not only good organizationally but they are true to the historical roots of the diocesan priesthood. We have a special bond with our bishop and with the fraternity of priests of our diocese. And this is an important element in our spirituality.

When we speak of the diocesan priest, we speak of one who has a commitment to his diocese, whatever form his ministry takes. This is the second element of our charism: *a call to the local Church.* We are living now with a renewed emphasis on the local diocesan Church, which is grounded in a tradition that goes back to the New Testament. Paul's letters were letters to local Churches. Vatican II defines a diocese as "a section of the People of God entrusted to a bishop to be guided by him with the assistance of his clergy so that, loyal to its pastor and formed by him into one community in the Holy Spirit through the Gospel and the Eucharist, it constitutes one particular Church in which the one, holy, catholic and apostolic Church of Christ is truly present and active" (*Decree on the Pastoral Office of Bishops in the Church,* No. 11). The diocese is a particular territory under the leadership of a bishop. The Council in the *Decree on the Ministry and Life of Priests* says: "All priests . . . are bound together by an intimate sacramental brotherhood; but in a special way they form one priestly body in the diocese to which they are attached under their own bishop. For even though they may be assigned different duties, . . . they fulfill the one priestly service for people" (No. 8). Priests assist the bishop in his work with the people of his particular territory, a diocese made up of parishes and religious communities. The word parish, since the year A.D. 150, has been an ecclesiastical term denoting an individual community or Church. The term pastor, which was originally reserved to the bishop, in the fourth century began to be used to designate the priest in charge of a small local community. The diocesan priest is called to be intimately involved with the people of a particular territory. We ordinarily make a lifetime commitment to serve these particular people. The exercise of this charism allows the whole world to be covered for Christ, for the whole world is to be divided into dioceses staffed by diocesan priests. Where the ordinary and staff are presently religious priests the aim is that eventually a local clergy will grow strong enough to assume responsibility for the territory.

The diocesan priest's mission is grounded in a diocese. We are primarily responsible for all the people and events within the local Church. Therefore, we do not follow our people if they move beyond our territory, our diocese. We wait to serve the new people who will take their place in our territory. We witness to the presence of Christ within a particular part of the world. But our concern does not stay only there. We share a concern for the universal Church, an extension of the bishop's concern for the whole Church. Our concern for the universal Church is a concern for the needs of other dioceses that are staffed by other diocesan priests; there is a bond of friendship and support as we share the same calling. We can be called "territorial priests," but our hearts are universal.

The third basic element in our charism is *a call to a special kind of community experience*. The diocesan priest has a call to community, but in a way different from that of a religious priest. The basic elements necessary for Christian community are a sharing of faith and life, mutual support and common prayer, and ongoing learning and outreach in service. When I asked diocesan priests who in their life offer them the opportunity to experience these realities, where do they find them, they listed the following: with priest friends, in support groups, at staff meetings, with priests in the house, among parishioners, with a spiritual director, in one's family, telephone conversations with friends, with the bishop, at educational programs, among lay friends, with the pastor, and at AA meetings. The diocesan priest, in searching for community, does not find it necessarily in the rectory. History gives us some examples of priests forming strong community in the rectory and then going on to establish a religious community. This may indicate that to seek to find the totality of his community experience or even his primary community in the rectory does not accord with the proper charism of the diocesan priest. It seems to me that our call to communal experience is a call to a sort of conglomerate community, a support system that is a cross section of the Church. This is seen in the responses I received, listing the people and events that supply the needs for community in diocesan priests' lives.

Evelyn Whitehead, in an article concerning ministers' needs for community, lists four basic communities that need to be in our lives: *the support community*, made up of those people who are concerned about us, in an ongoing way, as human beings, Christians, and priests; *a support network*, those special people that we call into our lives when there is a special need and concern, for example, a doctor-friend, a counselor, and the like; *the community of the place* where we live; and *the community of colaborers*, the people with whom we work. These are the four basic community experiences we have in our lives. No one grows without the support of community. Without community there is isolation, loneliness, and a loss of identity. However, the communal experience for the diocesan priest must be one that reflects and respects his special charism. It is created by many people, coming from various segments of his life.

The fourth element in the charism of the diocesan

priest is *a call to live the spirituality of the baptized believer, modified by the special vocation of priesthood.* Basic Christian spirituality consists in living the passion, death, and resurrection of Christ, which we have been brought into by baptism. The spirituality developed in the nineteenth century looked to the adornment of the soul. Emphasis was placed on the "battle" between vice and virtue. It was very individualistic in its orientation. Its quest for self-perfection led to a very static, unattractive, daily fidelity rather than a dynamic journey. An emphasis on introspection reluctantly allowed any involvement in the world. Such a training did not encourage us to respond to a call to community, a call to create a local Church, a call to fraternity with our brother priests and our bishop. A renewed spirituality, which is really a return to a more traditional spirituality, emphasizes relationship. The spiritual journey is to be lived out in relationship with the believing community. The Trinity is our ultimate exemplar. The need for dynamic growth is affirmed. Spiritual exercises can take on many different expressions. The basic conversion we seek is a greater sense of the presence of God, working in the present moment, in what we are actually doing, rather than in doing something additional. The journey is seen as a passage through various levels of a relationship, seeking quality, constancy, and depth rather than increased diversity or activity.

It was possible, and probably still is, to be a very passive priest and carry out daily spiritual exercises solely out of obedience or habit. It also is possible that the journey can be seen solely as a growth in knowledge. Theology, Sacred Scripture, and even Canon Law become the guides in an intellectual, or cerebral, development that does not affect the rest of our lives. What we want is, if I may put it this way, an experience of mutual respect between God and ourselves that leads to a greater intimacy, opening the door to a deeper sharing. This leads to a deeper affection and a desire for union that eventually opens out into that surrender which best expresses itself as: "Yes, here I am, Lord." This new emphasis in spirituality opens the door for us to see how connected our work is with our spiritual journey.

We have all heard that dictum from Thomas à Kempis: "Every time I go out among men I return less a man." As diocesan priests called to work among the people, because of some false attitudes inculcated in the course of our training, we have too often entered into our many diverse activities with a little voice whispering in the back of our head: "Every time you get involved with temporal affairs you are becoming less a man of God." This obviously leads to inner conflict. To avoid psychological stress or even serious damage, many of us have abandoned any hope of making progress on the spiritual journey, simply settling for the minimum requirements to do our work as best we can — but not feeling too awfully good about it.

A grace-filled moment for me came while reading a book by David Knight, *Lift Up Your Eyes to the Mountain*. It was in Chapter 7, concerning the desert and the city. Father Knight made a distinction between the call of the religious and the call of the laity. As I read the chapter I saw his comments on the laity very applicable to diocesan priests. To me it was clear that for us diocesan priests, spirituality must be grounded in the journey with our people in the place where we minister. Our path is one that makes its way through the city, along the valleys of life, and not ordinarily out into the desert or up to the mountaintops. Although, like Christ, there are times when we do need to go up into the mountains, like him we find our ministry and our spirituality grounded in involvement with people. We die to ourselves by becoming more deeply involved in their lives, transforming society by making it conform more to the ideal principles of the kingdom of God. What makes our involvement — our solidarity with life in society — transforming, is the faith, hope, and love that we bring to the risk that we take in this involvement. We mirror in our lives the concerns our people have in their lives. To wash

46

our hands of interest in any of the valid concerns of our people would be a message to them, loud and clear, that God is not present in those concerns — which would be certainly false. We are to experience the presence of God in and through the events and activities of the world. Our path is a committed path; we deliberately bring faith to the city, to all that awaits us there. We go into the city of humankind determined to choose to act in faith. At times, such a way of acting will not be acceptable and it will cost us much. Perseverance in this commitment is our way to grow in faith, hope, and love. It is in choices such as these, especially when they lead us into situations that are uncertain in regard to the outcome, that we experience most clearly the depth and reality of the presence of God in our lives. We are acting in the Spirit of the Gospel. Such risk is our way of renunciation; it is a dying to self to experience more fully the presence of God in our lives. It is a path that we must follow if we are to seek perfection in the biblical sense of that word. We want to set ourselves on this path with a conscious commitment to follow it all the way. Our spirituality as diocesan priests is very much with the people whom we are called to serve, walking among the ordinary events of each day, involving ourselves in the human situations of daily living. We find among our people a graced way where we are called to greater holiness, assisted by their call and their example. Living this experience, we gain a greater confidence in ourselves as spiritual guides among the people. Reflecting on these experiences in our lives, we are better able to help our people discover the presence of God in the experiences in their lives. Our spirituality is one with that of our people, with the added responsibility of calling them forth.

The fifth basic element in the charism of the diocesan priest is *to follow the spiritual tradition of the universal Church*, rather than some specific tradition within the universal tradition. There is a simplicity in the spiritual tradition followed by diocesan priests. It is grounded in the Scriptures and the Eucharist, in the word of God and the sacraments. By our calling, we do not adopt one particular spiritual tradition such as the Ignatian, Benedictine, or Franciscan. We follow the basic spiritual way of Christianity. The Eucharist and the word will always be primary for all. For diocesan priests there is no particular secondary thrust that arises from our vocation as such. The secondary elements in our lives come from the people we serve or from our own particular spiritual journey. We may have a spiritual director who is religious or we may have the custom of going on retreat to a particular religious center. We might have some special devotions that come from our upbringing. The richness of these experiences obviously will be shared with others in our ministry.

The sixth basic element in the charism of diocesan priests is that we are trained with a *primary emphasis on pastoral service* and one that will be colored by the local Church. The seminary training of diocesan priests is for the most part very pastoral. It should be adapted to the pastoral needs of our particular territory. We need to be encouraged to walk with our people. Some of the more basic job descriptions that have been developed for diocesan priests talk about our duties and our responsibilities in the area of liturgy, education, community and public relations, finance and administration, staff and parish management, personnel and personal spiritual life. All these areas should be basically covered with some experiential apprenticeship before ordination or certainly shortly after ordination.

There is much more I would like to share concerning each of these six elements, but that could be a book in itself. Because this explanation of the basic elements in our charism is an area that is new to diocesan priests, I would certainly encourage discussion of these six elements in our various support groups. Let us open and foster a conversation within which the Holy Spirit can further enlighten us. We have many special gifts that have not been tapped into yet. One of them is the gift of dialogue — dialogue among ourselves and dialogue between diocesan priests and religious priests about the journey of priesthood.

On a number of occasions there have been religious priests who have participated in this dialogue, and they usually respond that they do all the things that the diocesan priests do, especially those among them who are parish priests. So where is the difference? The difference lies not so much in what these men are doing as parish priests, but what their total religious community's charism is expressing. Many times their parochial involvement is an exception to the general charism of their own religious community. Even if their religious charism included parish ministry, this is not the same as being a diocesan priest. The primacy of the religious priest's commitment would not be to work in this particular local Church. His commitment would be to his religious community and its service in various local Churches.

Undoubtedly, much of what has been said about our charism as diocesan priests can, in some way, be applied to religious priests insofar as they are priests exercising ministry among the People of God. But it is difficult to make general applications in their regard, for there is such a rich variety among our religious brothers, their ministries, and their charisms. There are some religious institutes that are quite strictly societies of priests whose ministry is virtually coterminous with that of the diocesan priest. They would identify with us in far more ways than would those religious priests whose institutes are dedicated to special missions — not to speak of those priests whose institutes are wholly dedicated to the contemplative life.

Every priest who ministers to the people will do so in subordination to the bishop of the place, even the contemplative monk whose ministry is restricted to those who come to his monastery. Thus he will have a special union with the local bishop and with the other priests who minister in that diocese, at least for as long as he is ministering there. His union may be more ephemeral in comparison to the priest who is a member of the diocesan presbyterate, yet it cannot be something that is divorced from his spirituality. Every aspect of our lives has to be integrated into our response to Christ present in his many forms if we are to be truly holy men.

The religious priest then, in virtue of his priesthood and its expression in ministry, will have a certain relationship with the local bishop, with the priests of the diocese wherein he labors, with the people of that diocese, and with the local traditions, all of which will color his spirituality. His primary community will nonetheless remain that of his religious order or congregation. If he comes to a parish, he will usually come with some of his brother religious as a community. They will minister to the parochial community as a community, an exemplar and a nucleus, which will undoubtedly color the spiritual expression of the parish into which they enter even as they adapt to the traditions and customs of that parish. Tensions may arise out of these meetings of traditions, but for the most part we can hope it will be more a question of mutual enrichment. The more fully the religious priest as an individual and the religious community as a whole are living the charism of their particular religious vocation, the more fully will they bring their proper contribution to those communities and relationships they enter into in the course of their priestly ministry. It would be a real loss for everyone if the religious priest lost vital touch with his own community and charism and began to function like a diocesan priest. He can never really participate fully in the charism of the diocesan priest because he is not a fully committed member of the diocesan presbyterate. He would be a man without a powerful vision and source for his ministry.

We need to realize the splendor of the priesthood, and we need also to realize the special charism that each of us has as a diocesan or religious priest. We know we carry this special treasure in a vessel of clay — "Yet we who have this spiritual treasure are like common clay pots, in order to show that the supreme power belongs to God and not to us" (see 2 Corinthians 4:7) — and so we are bonded together in our human condition. The Curé of Ars said, "Do not be afraid of your burden, our Lord carries it with you." At times our human condition is a burden, and at other times it is a great joy. We all face difficulties at times concerning our health, our peace of mind, and our family commitments. We are concerned about the spirit of our priesthood, our awareness of our own poverty, the joy of discovering our weakness. We know the agony and the ecstasy in dealing with the People of God and with one another. We are sometimes overwhelmed by the negative forces in our world. Our heart goes out to those priests in other parts of the world who are persecuted and pressured on every side, who are suffering mental anguish, or incarceration, or even death. Within our own situation, we encounter criticism, bad faith, secularization, and rejection of the Christian message. We are sensitive to the growing tension that exists between the local as well as national Church and the Vatican, and the polarization that has taken place between the conservatives and liberals, the traditionalists and the modernists. All these elements weigh heavily on us and can begin to dominate our lives and our vision. They cannot be ignored, but they should not be overly stressed. They are part of a lived reality that needs to be balanced by being placed in a larger picture — within the large framework of Christ and his Church, as the sacrament of saving unity. We all need to back away at times to see the total picture.

As we look at our charism in context I think we also need to look at the evangelical virtues of poverty, chastity, and obedience. I would not have thought to bring them up at this point in our sharing except for an observation I recently heard. The observation was that if the spirit of poverty, chastity, and obedience is compromised, the very spirit and effectiveness of our ministry is compromised. A powerful statement! In the past, when I heard these three virtues mentioned, I always said to myself: "That's for the religious." That statement caused me to take a second look.

This is what the evangelical counsels say to me now:

Poverty speaks of responsible stewardship. I have gifts, gifts to be used in the service of the Lord. I am not called to be poor in the sense of lacking the things that make for a comfortable human life, though I do need to constantly guard myself from an undue affluence and a careless attitude toward the real needs of others. I am called very clearly to a spirit of poverty: to be ready to die to myself, my selfishness, in the use of my social, physical, intellectual, emotional, and spiritual gifts. Sometimes it is much harder to use these in a sharing way, for the benefit of others, than simply to give up the use of them. All too often we think of poverty only in terms of ascetic renunciation. The true spirit of poverty is found more in the acceptance of the ordinary in my own life. It is in making space, in a readiness to give of my time and forgo my own plans to be responsive to the needs and desires of others. My spiritual director in the seminary once told me that on reflecting back on his own life he was beginning to see that God's plan surfaced more in the interruptions of life than in the planned programs. We can truly die to self by letting go of our own plans, ever ready to be interrupted and surprised, and to go with the interruptions and surprises. This is spiritual poverty, to see this as part of the rhythm of our lives and not fight against it.

Chastity speaks of healthy relationships and of an integrated affectivity. We will talk about this more fully as we move along in this book. For now, it is important to see that the only way to grow is to come to terms with ourselves, the real self with the emotional life included, and to do this in a prayerful dialogue with the Lord. We need to know ourselves, especially our affective life and, confronted by this reality, to accept ourselves. It is okay to have all sorts of feelings. There is a Christian way to respond to them. In responding to them in that Christian way we can live through them, faithful to our commitments.

I hear *obedience* calling us to a healthy spirit of initiative and maturity in the use of our talents, a maturity that knows how to integrate this initiative into the common good, that is, ready to sacrifice for the common good. If we are not mature in our obedience, we can practice an unhealthy servitude or adopt an immature attitude toward authority figures. Only one who is weak in the possession of his own personhood needs to stand against authority to assure himself of his personal worth. When we have a good sense of ourselves we can meet authority in the person of bishop or superior as equal colaborers, seeking the same common good, and be ready to work out differences of vision and accept decisions without feeling violated or diminished in obeying.

The context for what we are about begins with a spirit of acceptance of ourselves and of one another. We want to see the value and the specialness that is there. Seeing these, we want to make opportunities for more communication among us, to talk about the specialness we see in ourselves and in one another and to bring this to prayer together so that the presence of the Lord might be felt even more strongly in the context in which he has called us to live our priesthood. This will enable us, not only with greater confidence but with more reality, to live our leadership role of being the sign of Christ the Head within our various communities, supported by all the facets of our particular charisms as diocesan or religious priests, as priests of Jesus Christ, our Lord.

3

Behind Closed Doors

Holiness, wholeness, integration, happiness, being who we are — these are all the same thing.

Christ Jesus, our Lord, though he may have come at the end of times, or in the midst of times, continues to be the summit, the crown, the end and reason for all times, the very purpose for all creation. He is the Father's delight and all that is, is for him, all is ordered to him, and is ultimately brought to oneness in him. "All things are yours, and you are Christ's, and Christ is God's." Our meaning, our being, lies in this. God had one design. Our essential grace and consecratedness comes from this. We were made, in God's design, to be Christ, to be intimately one with him in a oneness that finds its prototype in the oneness he has with the Father: "That all may be one as you, Father, are in me, and I in you; I pray that they may be [one] in us" (John 18:21).

In baptism, our consecratedness is recognized and given recognition in the community of the Church. In ordination, our consecratedness has been given a particular mode of expression in the conferral of an essential function within the Body, the People of God, along with the necessary powers to fulfill our role of headship in accord with the true nature of the Church. This is our essential being as priests. We find wholeness, happiness, and fulfillment only insofar as we live in accord with this our priestly being.

There are two fundamental elements here. First, there is the knowledge and understanding of the reality. As this is a reality that can only be known by the revelation — the perception of this graciousness of the creating, loving, paternal, divinizing God is beyond anything to which reason of itself could lead us: " '. . . no eye has seen, nor ear heard, nor the heart of man conceived, what God has prepared for those who love him' " (1 Corinthians 2:9) — it becomes ours by that reception of revelation which we call faith. Once we grasp this reality we are in the position, with the help of God's grace, to use our freedom to respond to it, the second basic element. This response is essentially love, a "yes" to God is a "yes" to the reality he has created and in which he expresses himself — expresses himself in self-gift as love.

This is what Paul is pointing to when he says: "The just person lives by faith." Without the reception of the revelation, without faith, we cannot be consciously alive to who we are. We can use our reason to attain to some understanding of our natural dignity as human beings. Others, by the way they live and act and by the way they respect us, can help us to understand our natural dignity. But only God can reveal to us the sublimity of the graciousness he has shown to us in the invitation he has given us in our creation to be intimately one with him in Christ. This is the end and purpose of our being as created by God, the potential of who we are. We will experience an endless frustration, however little we perceive its cause, if we do not respond to what our very being ardently seeks. The event of our priestly ordination, insofar as it irrevocably modified the way in which we were configured to Christ in baptism, modified the potency within us that must be fulfilled, if we are not to be constantly frustrated, unintegrated, lacking in wholeness, and therefore in holiness.

First, then, must come the perception of faith. And that perception must be constantly nurtured so that it is always vitally alive and growing, able to inform all our thinking and action. "Faith comes through hearing." Our faith is nurtured by an effective hearing of the word of revelation.

Since the revelation comes to us through and in the Church, this word is most powerfully and effectively spoken to us and able to be heard by us when the Church is gathered, when we are in community. Most especially is this so when that community is gathered for its most significant act and experience of itself in the celebration of the Eucharist.

I had the privilege to serve the Church at the Second Vatican Council. As a *periti* in the first session I knew the excitement of experiencing the Holy Spirit working in and through us in the elaboration of *The Constitution on the Sacred Liturgy*. Perhaps no other document of the Council has, so far, so touched the life of the Church as has this early document. For me, one of the most striking "words" of the Council is to be found in it: When the Gospel is proclaimed, Christ again speaks his saving word.

Ritual, when it is what it should be, when the rubrics are enacted with full meaning and spirit, gives a powerful, existential expression to reality. How often have you been touched by what takes place at the moment when we proclaim the Gospel at the Mass? We step into the pulpit and greet the people: "The Lord be with you." And they respond to us: "And also with you." Then we announce the event: "The Good News, the Holy Gospel according to Saint. . . ." And what then is the people's response? "Glory to you, O Lord!" And what do they cry at the end of the proclamation? "Praise to you, Lord Jesus Christ!" It is as though we had simply disappeared — or rather, our Christ person has become totally present. The people perceive, hear, and respond to "only Jesus."

The proclamation of the word will more effectively attain its purpose, the more fully we who enact it are in touch with this reality and enter into it.

The Old Testament and the New, the readings and the Great Prayer, in the context of the eucharistic assembly, powerfully proclaim the word of revelation, which engenders faith in all who have ears to hear. In all the gatherings of the faithful, more or less formal — the solemn celebration of the office, a liturgy of the word, a wedding or funeral service, a gathering in a sick room or two together in the reconciliation room, where the word is proclaimed by the Church — faith is effectively nurtured in all who hear. Even when we are the ministers who are proclaiming the word, we want also to be hearers who are hearing the word that brings faith.

When the proclaimed word is heard and received and allowed to come alive in our minds and hearts, then we can speak that word of faith which engenders and nurtures faith — whether it be the most formal of faith sharings when we as presidents of the assembly break the Bread of the Word in the homily or it be but one friend saying to another: "We can count on the Lord to take care of that," or a "God bless you" to the phone operator.

Looked at objectively, here is a rather strange phenomenon: Just men, who live by faith, and regularly ascend the pulpit to share their faith with even vast numbers, seem to find it exceptionally difficult to share faith openly, honestly, and frankly among themselves. Perhaps it is true for some of us that we never really do share faith, that our preaching is not a sharing of personal faith but an intellectual exercise, sharing ideas and concepts rather than our own lived experience of faith. As one parishioner commented: "We know what Father preaches all right, but we don't know what he believes." This could account for some of the ineffectiveness of our preaching. Those who preach only a word that is vitally alive in themselves are not only more effective preachers but usually have less hesitation about sharing faith with their brother priests. They spontaneously speak the word of faith with everyone. If we really know that the perceptions of faith can nourish, strengthen, encourage, and lift up the brother whom we love, then why are we so hesitant to express them? We are perhaps not so hesitant to share faith with the faithful, but we could also take a look and see what we are doing there.

"For where two or three are gathered in my name, there am I in the midst of them" (Matthew 18:20). We believe this — or do we? Would we ever ignore anyone else's presence in the way we so often ignore the Lord's? True — and this is very important: the Lord is in the other, and in us. In attending to the person who has come to us, we are attending to the Lord. In ministering to this sister or brother, we are the Lord. These are very "real presence." But should we not perhaps also give the Lord some explicit acknowledgment as the Third Party (or Fourth, or Fifth, or Sixth. . .) in our meeting? We can draw upon his healing love, his insightful wisdom, his joy, his open space for pure love.

Someone may counter at this point: "We have to be realists." Someone coming in to talk to us is not coming to be preached to. I would ask: "Does being realistic mean being real — responding to what really is? Is the Lord not really present with us?" How foolish then not to allow him to make the contribution that he can make, not to let his all-loving presence embrace our gathering.

It is a great help to keep the word of God present — his word is a real presence. We don't want to just leave it on the desk or tuck it in the shelf with so many other voices. It deserves to be in some way "enthroned" — given a fitting place so that it does announce to all his real presence, inviting us to invite him to add a word to the conversation.

It is surprising what an impact a little practice like this can have on our lives. I remember well a priest who was sent to the abbey on retreat many years ago. It was back in those times when a bishop would order such things. Father Ed had announced to his bishop his intention to resign from the priesthood. The bottle was getting to be too frequent a companion. He didn't want to go that way. But loneliness and sexual fantasies were sapping his morale. In the course of the retreat I had suggested bringing the Lord more into our lives by letting his word be a real presence in our rooms and in our offices as well as in our churches. I did not see Father Ed again for quite some time. I didn't expect to. I was honestly delighted when he walked into the retreat master's room not only in clericals but obviously very happy. He told me what had happened. When he got home after the retreat, he responded to the grace to carry through on this one little thing. He set out a table in his room and placed the open Bible on it. Each time he entered the room, there was the Lord, waiting to speak to him. An old friendship revived. Now Ed had just been appointed editor of the diocesan paper. He had a mission and a message.

One of our brothers who ministers in another ecclesial community shared with me a practice he has. He had gotten it from his mother. It is evidently fairly widespread among his brethren. They have what they call the "Bed Bible" — a Bible that is left open on the bed. As one retires, he has to pick it up and take the time to read a verse or two, receiving a word that will accompany him into sleep. He then sets the Bible on top of his shoes. In the morning as he reaches for his shoes he again encounters the Lord in his word. He receives a word or two to take with him through the day before he replaces the Bible on his bed. A very personal "Good night" — "Good morning" from the Lord, from the Friend. An adaptation of this for us might be to leave our breviary open on our desk or easy chair, letting the Scriptures of the day be there to speak to us. There is a sort of "virtuous" circle here. It takes faith to see the need and respond to the opportunities to nurture faith. That is why it is helpful for each of us to find the habitual little practices that will keep us nourishing our faith. A Bible lying open in an appropriate spot can be like a dish of candy on the coffee table, inviting us to nibble each time we pass by.

We cannot always join in a community gathering or even find a single person in order to hear a faith-building word, but it would be a rare occasion when we could not pick up a book and through its pages let the word of faith be spoken to us. The Sacred Scriptures, because of their special inspiration, will objectively always be the most powerful word for nurturing faith. But we do need various kinds of *sacred reading*, and each in its place will minister to us.

We need *sacred study*. We want to love the Lord our God with our whole mind, to seek him with all the power of our God-given intellects. We want to be always pressing our edges, entering more and more deeply into the understanding of the mysteries of faith. *Fides quaerens intellectum.*

We know painfully from our ministry what a great problem it is in our society to live this. Many of our people today enjoy the benefits of a good education that may well go on through high school to college and even to postgraduate work. And yet for all too many, faith education ends with First Holy Communion or Confirmation. If the just person is to live by faith, it means that every aspect of his or her life is to be informed by the living principles of faith. But how in the ordinary course of things can we hope that sixth-grade religion or even high-school CCD is going to be able to give direction and inner light to high levels of scientific and humanistic study? It just doesn't happen.

As priests our imbalance may be in the opposite direction. Our struggle to communicate the Gospel effectively is challenged by the need to speak into increasingly sophisticated contexts. We will in many more instances have to trust in the good will and judgment of our people as they make their own applications. Let us at least be sure we are well qualified in our own field. None of us would ever want to go to a doctor who was depending solely on what he learned in medical school even as little as five years ago. Nor would we want to entrust our case to a lawyer who was not keeping up with what is going on in the development of legal jurisprudence. It might cost us dearly. Yet what we minister to is far more important than physical health or a person's legal rights and pocketbook — though all of these are included within our concern. To seek to respond to today's pastoral needs solely with what the Spirit said to the Church yesterday will not be life-giving. We need to keep abreast with the development of doctrine and the signs of the times. And yet I wonder: How many of us have really absorbed the powerful and life-giving teaching of the Second Vatican Council, even as we celebrated its twentieth anniversary? I took the occasion to go back to *Gaudium et spes* and to look at it again with a couple of my confreres. What a revelation! We are all more aware of the breakthrough of the *Pastoral Constitution on the Church in the Modern World* renewing our understanding of the Church as the pilgrim People of God led by a collegial episcopate. But certainly no less significant is the call of the *Constitution on the Church* to renew our understanding of the human person as the image of God, with all the ramifications that this has on every aspect of human interaction, some of the more important of which the document spells out in detail. We need to sit down regularly with a man like Karl Rahner and let him lead us into the depths and then challenge us with the practical consequences of these theological realities. There are many good theological, scriptural, and pastoral periodicals available. It would be good to commit ourselves to read at least one of them regularly from cover to cover.

How much time can and should a busy pastor devote to keeping up-to-date theologically? How can he most effectively do this? My brother is a doctor. He is well supplied with cassette tapes from the different drug companies that seek to be of service to doctors by digesting and retailing current information. As he drives to his office or the hospital he listens to these tapes and thus makes use of this time to support his effort at keeping up-to-date. We priests might do the same. Sacred study can be fitted in. It is meant to serve. At times — a new significant pastoral comes from our bishops, an encyclical from Rome — we will have to carve out special time for sacred study. Yet, in general, we need to discipline ourselves to some steady updating.

If sacred study is geared to the intellect, we also need a reading that speaks to our wills, our hearts. I call this *motivational reading*. This probably corresponds most closely to what we usually mean when we speak of "spiritual reading." It will do us little good to know a lot and then do nothing about it. In fact, it will only make us more responsible for our lack of response. We need regular doses of that kind of reading that tones up our spirit and keeps alive in us the will to say "yes" to God's reality and promptings. How much reading? What subjects? Each of us needs to discern his own dosage. A good spiritual guide or friend can be helpful here as in so many other places along our journey. At times it will be our response to the more general or basic realities that we will want to have enlivened. At other times we will be more aware of particular needs: the Mass is just not speaking to us the way we want it to, we are struggling with prayer, or celibacy, or obedience, or social-justice issues, and on and on. We need motivation to effectively incorporate these values into our lives and into our ministry.

In regard to motivational reading we need to ask ourselves the practical question: "How much of this kind of faith nourishing do I need in order to keep fully alive, fully motivated to strive to be a total 'yes' to Reality?" The response will certainly vary, not only from person to person, but from season to season and crisis to crisis. Some liturgical seasons are so rich that if we enter into them we will find little need to seek any other motivation to be all there. But then there are the dog days of summer and perhaps even the doldrums of a long Lent. We need something more.

There is another kind of sacred reading. Rather than seeking to inform the intellect as does sacred study or move the will as does motivational reading, this reading seeks to open us to the experience of God. For a number of reasons I like to stick with the Latin name for this kind of reading: *lectio divina*. Our approach to this kind of reading will be different from the way we approach the other forms of sacred reading.

There is no pragmatism about *lectio*. It does not seek any results. *Lectio* is that time which we open to the Lord, when we say: "Speak, Lord, your servant is listening." And if he says it all in the first word, that is fine.

Scripture is the best for *lectio*, but it is not the only source. For many centuries most of the People of God could not read. They do seem to have generally developed their memories better than most of us. Having heard the word of God in the church they could call it up from memory. Not a few were noted as having the whole of the Bible at their disposal. All monks and clerics were expected to hold much of the Sacred Text in memory. Then there were the frescoes, already in the catacombs; they told the story of the Bible also. Later icons and other art forms developed until the whole of the Bible was depicted in medieval church windows. Beyond all this was the artistry of the greatest of artists, who painted large in his creation at the summit of which is enshrined the greatest of all icons, the very image of God: the human person. In all of these we can do our *lectio*, we can read God, we can experience God.

Fruitful *lectio* involves really a threefold process. First, we come into God's presence, calling upon the Holy Spirit. We depend on the Spirit, mindful of Jesus' words that he would send to us the Paraclete who would teach us all things, calling to mind whatever he has said to us. With the help of the Holy Spirit we open ourselves and make ourselves present, becoming aware of the Divine Presence in the medium of our *lectio* and in ourselves.

Then we listen. Some days we will listen to many words, we will look at many things, and the Lord will seem to remain silent — nothing is said to us. Other days, the first word will say it all, and we will rest in that word.

We do not determine the duration of our *lectio* by any results to be achieved (as we do with the other forms of sacred reading). The nature of friendship, of living life together, demands that we spend time like this. To ensure we do not get so caught up in doing the immediate that we do not make time for the important, we do want to set aside a minimum amount of time we will devote to *lectio* each day. At least five or ten minutes — but we are friends: who would not want more? A set time each day will help us to be faithful.

At the end of our allotted time, we thank the Lord. I never quite got over how wondrous it is that at any time we want we can sit down with the Lord and he will give us all the time we want and speak to us through his living word. We have near our monastery both a Hindu ashram and a Buddhist meditation center. Periodically one of the Hindus' or Buddhists' great teachers or masters will come to them for a visit. The announced visit creates great excitement. They invite us over and offer to bring their master to us. They are very excited because they are going to have the opportunity to sit for some hours or days at the feet of their master. And I think to myself: "Our Master is the one who made their masters, and we can sit at his feet whenever we want."

As we thank the Lord we take from our encounter a "Word of Life" so that the loving Presence may go with us, illuminating our way.

Some days, when we sit at our *lectio*, the Lord will speak a word to us. We have all had the experience. He says something and it abides with us for hours, days, weeks, years, forever. We do not have to "take" a word — it is given to us. It is a moment of grace. On the other hand, some days the Lord seems to be singularly absent. On these occasions we do need to take a "word": a single word, or a phrase, or a sentence — a pithy capsule that will nourish us and others whom we will meet on our journey that day. If each day a word of the Lord comes alive in us, we will come to have more and more the mind of Christ.

Before moving on, let me sum up this simple method of daily *lectio*:

LECTIO DIVINA

1. Take the Sacred Text with reverence, acknowledging God's presence, and call upon the Holy Spirit.
2. For ten minutes listen to the Lord and respond to him.
3. Thank the Lord and take a "word" with you.

One of the reasons I prefer to use the Latin name for this simple form of experiential reading is that the name has always implied the whole of what is a rather natural process which the tradition has summed up in the four words: *lectio — meditatio — oratio — contemplatio.* When the monastic horarium (or daily schedule) assigned time to *lectio* or a priest sat down to his daily *lectio*, it was not a question so much of sitting down to read as it was taking time to enter into this process. On a given day he might actually spend much of the allotted time reading; on another day he might read very little, moving quickly along in the process.

The purpose of *lectio* is to enter into the experience of God. A "word" comes alive for us, we respond — the communication becomes communion, union. In *lectio* we open our inner ear to let God speak a "word" to us. Then we let that word come alive in us.

In our more recent tradition, "meditation" has meant a discursive process, which might also harness the energies of the imagination and emotions. We took a word of revelation and used our faculties to do all that we could to enter into the full meaning, to break open the nut, as one of the patristic images would have it, to get at the meat within.

Basically there are two approaches to meditation: the effortful and effortless. We find them in every tradition. For example, in Zen there is Rinzi Zen, which adopts a rigid meditation posture while the mind works ceaselessly with a given koan (for example, "What is the sound of one hand clapping?"), seeking to break through the impossible statement to the being that is beyond. Soto Zen adopts a more supple posture and the mind lets go by watching the breath or counting backward or employing some other simple technique. In our Christian tradition we find these same two approaches. Discursive meditation is full of effort, using all the faculties, seeking to make a breakthrough to the reality beyond the concepts. On the other hand, the more common meditation method of an earlier time simply let the word be present, perhaps gently repeating it mentally or even verbally, until, as the tradition would express it, the mind descended into the heart, until the word formed the heart.

In Saint Luke's Gospel we read more than once that Mary "pondered all these things in her heart." I was absolutely dismayed by a recent translation that betrayed this by saying she thought all these things over. The Greek word implies the idea of letting the experience simply rest there, letting its weight *(pondus)* make an impression upon — that is, form — the heart. *Lectio, meditatio, oratio, contemplatio* — this is one of the most traditional ways in our Christian tradition for summing up the journey in prayer, the way of Christian spirituality, of growing in union with Christ.

In the process of *lectio*, the received word is allowed to abide — through gentle presence or repetition — until it makes its impression on the heart and calls forth a response: prayer. According as to how the word impresses us, it is a prayer of adoration, thanksgiving, petition, reparation . . . an affective prayer. When the word so impresses us that our response is total, we are in contemplation: the lover's complete surrender.

One of the things that is evident in this quite natural process is that there are two involved here. We open to receive a word. The Word who speaks the word does the rest as we remain open and responsive. A more active or effortful method of meditation can become too much our own project, forming the false self rather than opening the self to formation by the other, turning into ourselves instead of turning into God.

Words, words, words — sometimes we wonder if we can say another word of prayer. We are disgusted, not with prayer, but with prayers. Our lives are so filled with them. When we do finally go into our room and close the door to speak to our Father in private, the last thing we want is more words.

This is the natural course of any developing relationship. At first a lot of words have to be used as we seek to get to know about each other. As the relationship develops we have less to say. It is more important to be together, doing things: actions speak louder than words. If the relationship is allowed to develop to the level of intimacy, we come to the time when we need to leave off speaking and doing and just *be* to each other. This reaches its crowning moment in the marital embrace. In Scripture, God repeatedly employs the image of marriage to convey to us the kind of intimacy he wants with us.

When we go into our room to pray, if we have been fed by the Scriptures, if we have been talking with and about the Lord, doing things all day with and for him, we are ready for and want to enter into the final phase of the process, the *contemplatio*.

Unfortunately, many "active" priests harbor the prejudice that contemplative prayer is only for the chosen few, for monks and nuns, not for the man who is busy about many things. This false idea perhaps goes back to seminary days. One priest told how in their course of ascetical and mystical theology, when they had finished the section on ascetics the priest-professor closed the book saying: "The rest of this has no meaning for you; if perchance you are appointed chaplain to the Carmelites you can look it up." Thus many good priests keep laboring at active prayer when in fact they desperately want the refreshment that comes from contemplative prayer, a refreshment that is due them. Recently a priest came to see me; actually he was a bishop, a humble, gentle man. Exceptionally faithful to the Lord, for over forty years he had never missed his daily visit, his time with the Lord. It had been hard, but he had kept at it. Now he was expansively joyous. A few months before he had accidentally come upon Centering Prayer. The years of labor ended for him as he opened space and the divine love swept in. How wonderful! And how sad that he had had to wait over forty years for such refreshing prayer. This is not an uncommon story among priests in ministry — someone failed to share the secret, the key.

Our Lord said, "Come to me, all who labor and are heavy laden, and I will give you rest" (Matthew 11:28). Prayer should be refreshing. When we go into our room, close the door, and pray to our Father in secret, it should be a time of great refreshment. Certainly not just another duty. (A marriage will not do well if the partners are resigned to doing their duty and rendering the marriage debt!) Once the relationship has been well established — and that should take place in the seminary if not before — our time of private prayer should be the time for enjoying and growing in that relationship.

If we have not been accustomed to doing this: sitting down and quietly opening ourselves to the Lord and enjoying his presence and love — in faith, of course — we will probably at first find it somewhat difficult. If we have been on the go, go, go, it is difficult to let go. This is where one of our traditional methods, like Centering Prayer, can be of great help.

The name "Centering Prayer" is a fairly new label (coming from Thomas Merton) for a very ancient method of *contemplatio.* After we have settled ourselves quietly (sometimes a little exercise or stretching is helpful here) and closed our eyes gently, we simply turn in faith to God dwelling in us and in love we give ourselves to him. These twenty minutes are all his. He can do with us whatever he wants. If he wants to leave us just sitting there like a bump on a log, that's OK. How often have we left him sitting, waiting for us? We will be refreshed in the quiet sitting. There are two kinds of love: the love of enjoyment and the love of desire. This quiet waiting is the love of desire. He lets us grow, opening more space in us, so that he can then give us more of the other, the love of enjoyment, the joy in his presence.

In order to remain quietly there, we use a prayer word or rather a love word — perhaps our favorite name for him, or whatever expresses our being to him in love. The trouble with us celibates is that we haven't made love enough, so we are a bit inept here. In the embrace, even a mere sound can become the code of communion.

We are there with him. The rest is his doing. We rest — in his love — and he does the rest. We let him take care of his world for twenty minutes (believe it or not, he can manage it without us for twenty minutes — and not make too much of a mess of it!) and take care of us. We become that little child who enters the kingdom, the lover of the Canticle or Hosea (Osee), and rest in his love. He has what he wants and that is all that matters.

It is a healing time, of making oneself whole again. All sorts of things come up. We just let them go, returning gently to him with our love word. Hurtful memories with all their hurt rise and pass away. It is a time of forgiveness and reconciliation. The tensions of the hour grab at us and we let them go, finding the freedom that will let us face the problems after the prayer with new freedom and creative energy. Bright ideas come along and we let them pass, too. They will be there later when we need them for ministering or preaching. For now, we are content with the poverty of a single word of love. Indeed, we use the word only when we need it to return gently to the silent presence. It is simply a time of love, of being with the Lord.

Be good to yourself, for God's sake, and twice a day give yourself this time of intimacy. Let him refresh you, energizing you at the beginning of the day, picking you up again toward evening. He can manage the world, not to speak of the parish, for those twenty minutes. In fact, you might find he does some pretty wonderful things while you are "wasting time" with him in refreshing prayer.

Let me sum up this ancient, ever-new, simple method for entering into *contemplatio*:

CENTERING PRAYER

Sit relaxed and quiet.
1. Be in faith and love to God who dwells in the center of your being.
2. Take up a love word and let it be gently present, supporting your being to God in faith-filled love.
3. Whenever you become *aware* of anything, simply, gently, return to the Lord with the use of your prayer word.

After twenty minutes let the Our Father (or some other prayer) pray itself.

As I mentioned I recently returned again to *Gaudium et spes*. I hadn't read it in quite a few years. I was struck by how this doctrinal study that was concerned with the insertion of the Church into the modern world so took it for granted that contemplation was a part of this. And it wasn't addressing itself to canonical contemplatives or specially consecrated religious, but to every member of the Church. It noted, in particular, that we cannot hope to keep our perspective in this world of intense activity and glut of specific knowledge without an ability to contemplate. It stressed the need of contemplation to keep us free from the bondage of material things. Contemplation alone can keep us alive to the wonder of our own being, the image of God, and of the whole of his creation. It preserves us as persons in the face of the collective. So says the Spirit speaking through the Council.

If contemplative prayer is something new for us, at first we might just experience an increase of peace and joy, some release of tensions; but if we stay with our practice, we will come to see all the fruits of the Spirit mature in our lives. Others will probably notice them even before we do. I hesitate to make further claims in regard to the fruits of the prayer. The working of the Spirit is very subtle. As one priest wrote after some years of centering: "About the prayer, all I can say is that when I miss it, I miss it."

We have touched on a number of things in this chapter. How does one manage the juggling act — how do we get all these things into our already overly active and full lives?

It is not easy to implement practically our priorities so that we do the important — what is important to us as priested men: keeping fully human, meeting our physical needs, keeping intellectually and culturally alive, nurturing our spiritual growth, preparing homilies well, etc. — rather than being wholly consumed with doing the immediate: answering phones and doorbells, doing secretarial work and household tasks, running errands, and so on. There is a time for doing these things, especially doing them with others, doing them with and for God who is in them all. But it is a false sense of ministry to think we should always be available for these things to the extent that they are allowed to squeeze out completely the important things. Something that can help us to see our priorities clearly and to respect them in the way we live is to have our own *rule of life*.

We have different instinctive reactions to that little word "rule." Some of us love rules. We find a great joy in keeping rules; a certain security and sense of accomplishment or devotion is found in fulfilling them. A rule of life can be a source of additional joy — though care must be taken not to make too much of rules. Some of us, though, experience a very negative reaction when we think of rules. They loom up before us as cages, or spikes that nail us to a wall and conform us to someone else's idea of how our lives should be shaped. Or they become instruments of self-torture, producing all sorts of guilt. It is difficult for us to challenge ourselves with the call of our rich potential and not at the same time induce guilt in ourselves because we fail to live up to so much of our potential, to hold fast to an ideal that is big enough to ever call us forth and simultaneously to lovingly embrace the reality of who we are here and now, where we actually are on our journey. A rule of life should never be a cage or a cross, but rather a trellis.

I love flowers. One of my more refreshing avocations is to putter around the flower beds. A healthy climbing rose is a real challenge. It seems to have energies unlimited. Nonetheless, no matter how high it climbs, it yet needs support; otherwise it will fall back on itself and its growth will be truncated, its blossoms fewer. Most of the time the climbing rose is reaching out in all directions — all directions of up — but at certain points it needs support or it will fall back. With proper support, there is no limit to the heights it will attain, to how much beauty it will bring into the world.

This is how I see a rule of life: a trellis that supports us when and where we need it so that we can go ahead with untrammeled growth, being to our people a beautiful expression of the unlimited love of God.

Let me suggest a practical way to go about formulating for ourselves a personal rule of life, one that will support us in being all that we want to be, all that God wants us to be.

First, I think we need to stop and tune into the Holy Spirit. " 'What no eye has seen, nor ear heard, nor the heart of man conceived, what God has prepared for those who love him,' God has revealed to us through the Spirit" (1 Corinthians 2:9-10). If we try to construct a rule on our own, we are apt to create one that is far too small, that does not really support us in being all that God wants us to be as his sons enlivened by his Spirit. Throughout this whole process we want to be listening to the Spirit as she speaks to us through our own lived experience illumined by our theological understanding.

Attuned to the Spirit, then, and to our own deep spirit, let us first write down *what we want to get out of life*. What do we want? What are our goals, our aims, our hopes, our ambitions? Long range and short range. Sublime and prosaic. To be a saint and to play the guitar. To really get into contemplative prayer and to shave ten points off our golf score. To lose thirty pounds and to have a better relationship with Mother or Dad. . . .

Ultimately, we all want happiness. But what is happiness? The comic-strip character Charlie Brown has some good definitions. We all probably have a few pet ones of our own. The happiness we are talking about here, true happiness, does not lie in the emotions or feelings. It is good to have happy feelings and emotions. I am not knocking that. But true happiness, the deep happiness that is the fruit of the Spirit, holy joy, is quite compatible with some very real pain, hurt, and sorrow. True happiness lies in knowing what we want and knowing we have it or are on the way to getting it. Most people are unhappy because they do not know *what they really want*. Part of this is not being in touch with the true self, the deep connatural aspirations of our being, that being which is not only the very image of God, and therefore has divine aspirations and needs, but also has been Christed in a special way in baptism and ordination. We need to be in touch with these needs and respond to them or we will constantly experience frustration. We need also to be willing to make choices where choices have to be made. When we are unwilling to limit our freedom by choosing particular options, letting go of others, we become prisoners of our own freedom. Only when we decide what we want, where we want to find our happiness, can we hope to experience true happiness. So our first task is to get in touch with what we really want.

With a list of these in hand, we are ready for the second step. We now want to make a realistic inventory of *what we have to do to attain what we want*. Here we need to be very practical. We want to look at our very basic physical needs: how much sleep do I need to function happily as a human person (every good rule of life begins with going to bed!), how much food, exercise, etc.; our human needs: relaxation, friendship, reading, study, and so forth; and our Christ-needs as men with a

73

special being in Christ: prayer. sacred reading, sacraments, and the like.

As a help toward making this inventory more realistic and complete we can, as a third step, take a look over our shoulder. In the last six months or so, *what has kept me from being who I want to be, doing what I want to do?* Certainly, there will come up here things within myself which I can address, places where, perhaps, I have to make some difficult choices or practice a little more discipline if I want to get what I want out of life. There will, undoubtedly, also be things in others' life situations and in my own that militate against my personal goals. Here I will pray the serenity prayer: "God, grant me the serenity to accept the things I cannot change, courage to change the things I can, and wisdom to know the difference."

With all this data I am now ready for the most difficult part: *actually formulating my rule of life on a daily, weekly, and monthly basis.* For some, a sort of horarium works — provided that we keep in mind we are talking about a trellis; we will be away from it more than we will be attached to it, but it will be there to fall back on to support our going in the direction we want to go. Up at six, exercise and shower, meditation at six-thirty, dress, morning prayer at seven, preparation for Eucharist, celebration or breakfast at eight depending on scheduling, etc. Perhaps many will not find any kind of horarium realistic for the hectic life of ministry or for their particular temperament and way of functioning. A schedule for them will have to take the form of something like six hours of sleep, half-hour exercise, office, ten minutes of *lectio*, two periods of meditation, etc. — a sort of checklist, things fitting in where they can be fit in. I know some secular institutes for priests use this method. There will be elements that will fit in on a weekly program: an afternoon with friends, three hours at the gym, two hours of theological study, meeting with our support group, and so on.

I think an important element of life is a monthly day

of retreat, or at least a half day — in other words, some time regularly to take a look at one's life. We can get awfully pushed around by circumstances, people, things. If we let this go on and on, it can lead to a profound despair. If we are not happy, if we don't see our life going in the direction we want it to go, we shouldn't just keep pushing along. We need to stop and take inventory.

If there are elements in our lives that we do not like, we should see if there is something we can be doing about eliminating them. Let us not fall back into the "victim soul" complex. Such might give us an easy (though phony) excuse for not performing the way we need to, but in the end we ourselves are truly the victims of such excuses. If, in fact, there are things about which we can do nothing (we shouldn't be too quick to decide this is the case — though we are all painfully aware it sometimes obviously is), then we should be sure to see that these things are part of the price we have to pay in this very imperfect world in order to attain what we really want to attain, to be who we really want to be, so that it is worth putting up with them. Thus we find a certain happiness in allowing even these things to be in our lives.

A monthly retreat can be a time of joy as we see that our life is going in the direction we want it to go. It will usually be a moment to refurbish our rule of life, for life is constantly changing and so must our rule be undergoing constant change if it is going to be truly adapted to our lives and supportive of them. If the rule isn't really helping, throw it out. We certainly do not need any extra baggage to keep track of. A particular friend, one who is willing to walk with us in openness on our journey, confessor or not, might serve us as well as a rule of life. Our monthly retreat might be getting together with this friend. We will talk more about friendship later.

The point here is that we are literally made to be happy. I get in trouble from time to time for some of the things I write. Once I got rather heated responses for writing that one of the most pernicious heresies I know of I learned from the *Baltimore Catechism*. The "heresy" was a question that asked: "Why did God make me?" And the response, as I recall it, was that "God made me to know, love, and serve him in this world and to be happy with him in the next." Besides being a bit incomprehensible (I don't know how you love someone and not be happy with him), it leaves a rather undesirable image of God, a God who wants only service here and happiness only later on. No, God wants us to be happy with him at every moment, here and hereafter — just as any lover would.

Yes, there is the cross. Mortification is an essential part of any Christian life. But it is not something added on, some medieval practice of hair shirt or whip, nor is it a pebble in the shoe or skipping a dessert (although our health may require the latter). Mortification is "making dead" or actually seeing as dead (as it really is) all the falseness and phoniness in our lives. Most especially, dying to the false self, that self we are led to fabricate, the self made up of what we have, what we can do, what others think of us — a construct outside ourselves, fragile, defensive, competitive. Mortification, more positively, is the blood, sweat, and tears that go into doing what we need to do to be true to ourselves as Christed men, signed with that special character of ministry. To live for others — first of all for Christ so that he can live again in us for others — and to live for ourselves in such a way that we are able to bring to others all that we truly are: this is the daily, hourly, moment-to-moment cross that is truly redemptive, that is powerful, and in which or on which we do find joy because it is what we want as disciples of Jesus Christ.

There is a paradox here, of course. Any one of us who has looked at a crucifix and realized that that man hanging there in agony is the all-glorious Son, Second Person of the Trinity, has glimpsed what is at the heart of this paradox. This is surely one of the reasons why we need daily *lectio*, daily *meditatio*, daily *contemplatio*, to be able to live in this realization so that we can be men of fundamental joy and hope even as we walk (or crawl at times) in compassion with a humanity so sorely wounded by inhumanity.

We are sinners. We know it. To come to that wholeness that is holiness we need healing. But the healing takes place in the very process of daily living who we are. For us as priests that means ministry, first ministering to ourselves as much as necessary in order to be able to minister to others. The Council of Trent insisted we needed first some years of seminary training before we attempted to minister to others. Most today would accept that without question, at least in regard to the intellectual formation. We need to hang on to the priority expressed here. We need first to take care to prepare ourselves for ministry before undertaking it. That is a priority which needs to stand even in our daily lives. We humbly face our actual limitations — we can do only so much in a twenty-four-hour day with our given talents and energies — and ask others to accept them, not giving in to the myth of total availability. If we are going to love our neighbor as ourselves, we better be sure first that we do love ourselves and take good care of ourselves, responding to our own needs for happiness so that we can labor effectively with and in the Lord for the happiness of our sisters and brothers.

Our quest for personal holiness, our personal prayer, our physical, emotional, and intellectual well-being — none of these can be seen apart from our ministry as priests. Nor can our ministry be seen as apart from them. All are intimately interconnected. If there is not a deep substratum of peace and joy in our lives, then I think we need to stop and come home to ourselves and see where the connections are broken, where the flow of the Spirit is being interrupted. But if these fruits of the Spirit are present, then what we are doing is well. We can call ourselves priests, through and through. We have every right to be deeply, quietly happy, even in the midst of our daily struggle and our ministry to the struggles of others.

4

It's the Mass
That Matters

●

I always tell people when they invite me to visit them that I never forget an invitation. That was the case when the spiritual director of Huntington, the major seminary on Long Island, was saying good-bye at the end of his retreat at Saint Joseph's Abbey: "Come any time you can; we will be glad to pick you up at the airport." In actual fact, I did not have much of a chance to forget his invitation. Two weeks later I found myself unduly delayed by snow in Chicago. It looked as if I would get into New York late, much too late to make my connection to Massachusetts. So I called Father, reminded him of his kind invitation, and asked if he could put me up for the night, or what might remain of it by the time I reached New York. I hadn't averted to the fact that Huntington is a good seventy-five miles from the airport. True to his word, Father was there, at two in the morning and in spite of some heavy snow, to meet me.

Late that morning, after a good sleep, I was invited to celebrate the Eucharist with the students and then meet with the deacons after lunch. It was to be just an informal get-together, my responding to whatever they would like to talk about. As the sharing went on, one of the deacons said: "You know, Father, your Mass was different." We were then in the very beginning of the transition. The altar had been turned around, but very little else had changed. Most of us priests were still very conscious of rubrics and our obligation to carry them out to the letter. I wasn't sure what I had done that was "different," but I was prepared to say something to the effect that we Cistercians do have our own rite — that might account for the difference. Nonetheless, with some curiosity I made bold to ask: "What was different about it?" I have never forgotten the deacon's response: "You really spoke to the Father."

At the altar, perhaps more than any other place, we enter formally into our role as men ordained to make present the headship of Christ. To fulfill this role most effectively we need to have a deep experiential union with Christ, the kind of union that comes about only through deep personal prayer. We also need to be intimately related with our people — related as intimately as the Head is with the rest of the Body. The assembly of people and the priest, together as one, celebrate the Eucharist, each fulfilling his or her proper role within the celebration. In the pre-Vatican II liturgy it was easy to conceive of the priest as being the one chosen from among the people to go before the Lord in their behalf as their mediator. We had lots of props: altars raised high, rich vestments, attending ministers, ringing of bells and even, at times, clouds of incense. The priest stood apart from the people, in front of them, ahead of them, above them, his back to them, approaching God, often present in an impressive eucharistic tabernacle or throne. The priest was very obviously the mediator.

Today, the emphasis has changed. The priest is in the midst of the people. Altars are less and less raised on high. They have rather been brought low. Vestments have been greatly simplified, a simple sign of office. Ministers rise, so to speak, from among the people, rather than apart from them. Bells are little heard and incense has all but disappeared (though we will probably see some return of these things). The priest is obviously one with his people, face-to-face with them, speaking directly to them. (I wonder now how I could ever have solemnly chanted the Gospel to the north wall in an unknown language and thought that that was a proclamation of the Good News. Where was I?)

The shift is important, very important. The mediator was getting too far away from the people to be relevant to them. The people need to know we are indeed one with them. And we need to know that, too. But the people also want to know, need to know, that we are one with God. Today, as we stand there, face-to-face with the people, it is not easy to deceive them. Most of the props have fallen away. We have to stand on our own two feet, in our own reality.

When the new liturgy was first taking hold, I had the occasion to visit the aged mother of one of our monks. Mother Gossman was eighty-six years young, blind for many years, but very lively and sharp. She still sang the songs of her girlhood to me with obvious relish and merriment. We were discussing the new form of the sacrament of reconciliation. Mother loved the changes. But she had the wisdom that comes with years: "It's not going to be easy for them [the priests]; they really have to be there now." What she saw to be true in the new face-to-face encounter within the sacrament of reconciliation is certainly true also of the eucharistic celebration.

There is little hope that we can really speak to the Father at the altar if we have not gone into our rooms, closed the door, and spoken to him in secret. The Father can be no stranger to us. He has to be our Father, a Father with whom we are on very good terms so that we can, publicly, dare to say: "We come to you, Father . . .

Father, you are holy indeed ... Our Father." As our Lord tells us, "No one knows the Father but the Son and those to whom he reveals him" (see Luke 10:22). We need to spend a lot of time with the Son, letting him reveal the Father to us — getting to know the Father through the Son and spending time with him in deep prayer, like Centering Prayer. Father — Abba — becomes also our prayer word; it becomes as natural to us as it is to Christ, because through our communing with Christ our essential identity with him becomes a living reality on all levels of our being.

Our people want to sense that we are deeply one with Christ our Head and with him speaking to the Father — but also one with them, knowing, understanding, and loving them in a caring way. Just as they will sense that we are really able to be to God for them because we are able to speak directly to the Father, so also they will know we are really with them because we speak directly to them. Our sincerity and our directness need to reach them. This is not the easiest thing to do when a good part of the time we have to read texts, texts that become all too familiar by constant repetition.

I think it is extremely important that we make full use of the options the rubrics give us when we are celebrating the Eucharist with our people. Adaptation is essential when leading a community in worship. If we start off the Eucharist all the time by simply reading one of the formulas printed in the book or reciting one we have committed to memory, we certainly are not starting off on the right foot. We don't talk to people whom we love that way, people whom we are glad to see. There are a number of places where the rubrics tell us to speak to the people "in these or similar words": at the beginning of the celebration, whether we are blessing holy water or using a penitential rite, and again when we ask the people to bring the offertory rite to a completion by their fervent prayer. When we invite the people to join in the Lord's Prayer and then in Communion are two other places where we can speak to them directly out of the fullness of our own hearts, the texts in the missal just guiding us in the basic sentiments we need to express. The ritual actually leaves us space for even more spontaneity in inviting us to make some brief remarks at the beginning of the celebration, before the readings, calling for the general intercessions rightly called "the prayer of the faithful," entering into the anaphora and finally at the dismissal. Thus we do have ample opportunity in every celebration to repeatedly speak to the people in a very direct and personal way.

The way we read the Gospel and the other readings — if we don't have a deacon and readers, we should, of course, make every effort to assure their participation — will very quickly tell the people whether this Good News is something that really lives in us, that we believe and want to share, or if it is just so many unfamiliar or too familiar words. The in word today is "proclaim." It is a good word. It conveys deep conviction and real desire to communicate. That is what should mark the Scripture reading. It will, but only if we have spent enough time with the readings so that the Spirit who lives in them has had an opportunity to come alive within us. No matter how good our elocution, if the word does not live within us it will never be proclaimed in a lively way, in a way that engenders life. It will have to work in spite of us instead of through us, empowered by the life within us.

With the homily, one with the proclamation of the Gospel, the Liturgy of the Word comes to its consummation. Here the priest as presider most properly exercises his role in the Liturgy of the Word. If our homily is closely tied with the Scriptures, it will have power because of the Scriptures. It will have warmth and feeling; it will evoke an effective response, being an agent of transformation in the lives of the hearers, if it flows from the Scriptures as they truly live within us, warming our hearts and transforming our lives. Only fire, albeit the steady radiance of glowing coals, can start fire. Our words do not always have to be flaming, but they do have to have fire within them; otherwise they are as effective

82

as a spent fire, a heap of ashes. Our fire must come from the Holy Spirit who has had time in prayer to call to our minds all that Jesus has said to us.

Carl told me of a meeting of the ministerial association in his area. The host, the pastor of the local Presbyterian church, shared his procedure for the preparation of the Sunday sermon. He told his audience that on Tuesday he read the text for Sunday from all available translations, selected the translation that spoke the message clearest, and that evening meditated on it. On Wednesday he studied commentaries on the texts, made an outline, then wrote the first draft of his sermon. On Thursday he edited this draft and then went to the pulpit to deliver it, taping his delivery. Next he listened to the tape. On Friday he wrote the final text and gave it to the church secretary to type so that the congregation could receive copies after Sunday service. On Saturday, he went into the pulpit again with his text in hand and delivered the sermon, making appropriate marks for emphasis, etc. Then came the moment of truth. The pastor looked at Carl and asked, "Carl, what is the Roman Catholic priests' way of preparing the Sunday message?" I have to confess, as I heard the story I found my defenses arising. We wouldn't have to go to all those translations; we would go to the original Greek and Hebrew. Those Protestants aren't properly trained. We wouldn't get glued to some prewritten text. We would preach out of the fullness of the moment, leaving room for the Spirit. But deep down, I knew it was a cover-up. We don't use our Greek and Hebrew. We don't use what we learned in the seminary. Nor do we give all that much time for the Spirit to enlighten us so that we can in truth preach with the power of the Spirit.

I like an illustration Werner Erhard used in speaking to priests and ministers. He had found many of them to be like a man who goes into a restaurant and studies the menu with its descriptions of all the fine dishes offered, and then, instead of ordering one of the dishes to experience it, he eats the menu. If all we serve up to our people are ideas, words, and concepts and do not bring them into a shared *experience* of God and his Good News, they will go away as nourished as if we had served them a menu instead of a meal.

We need to know to whom we speak as well as of whom we speak. We need to be concerned with their concerns. For successful writing I find it is necessary to have something I really want to say and someone to whom I really want to say it. If I write without conviction, just passing on someone else's words, or write into a void, just to write and not to really communicate with someone, my writing will be dead. I believe the same is true for homilies. We need to stay with the readings until they give us something we really want to say. We need to know and love our people with all their concerns and really want to share with them what we have received. I don't think we can depend on this kind of communication emerging spontaneously. Once the message of the readings has taken hold of us, we need to spend time quietly, in imagination as it were, certainly in spirit, with our people, listening to their hearts, and our own hearts, so that we can see how to bring our word of life into those hearts precisely as the word they want and need to hear. The Holy Spirit with her gifts of wisdom, understanding, and counsel has an important role to play here.

As we bring the Liturgy of the Word to a fruitful completion let us not break the flow of the experience by interjecting extraneous announcements. The rubrics open the space for a presidential word at the time of the dismissal. This is the time for announcements. This is where most of them really fit. As we send the people forth these announcements are part of the way that they can bring the Eucharist into their active lives. If the activities we are announcing don't in some way flow out of the life of the eucharistic community, it probably is not appropriate that they be announced at the gathering. Certainly our announcements will be more effective if we do see the connection and help our people to see the connection.

Another place we need to make the connection is in regard to the collection. The collection should be a real part of the Eucharist, the way in which the people bring to Christ's sacrifice the sacrifices of their own lives sacramentally represented in the fruit these sacrifices have produced. I think we could take a lead here from our Protestant brothers and sisters. In their services the collection is not just something that is sort of slipped in while the service goes on. It is an integral part of the service, introduced by the president, standing in its own rite, with nothing else going on while it is taking place. It is usually concluded with the ushers bringing the offerings solemnly to the president, who receives them in the name of the Lord or holds them up before the Lord. A little time and attention here can make the offering much more meaningful for our people and make it more integrally a part of the offertory.

Incidentally, I noticed in the Orthodox Church the priest makes it a point to place his own offering on the plate. This is another way in which the priest can further his identification with his people.

With a little effort we can help the people to sacramentalize all that surrounds the eucharistic celebration and make it a much more integrated experience for them and for their lives. We will do this most effectively if we have in fact done this for ourselves. The coming to church can be seen as the gathering of the People of God, not just a utilitarian thing that has to be done, but a sacramental act that can grow in significance.

The church itself can be more fully experienced as our Father's house. We are at home there. We can be there to welcome the people as they arrive, encouraging them to welcome one another. Let there be warmth and spontaneity and celebration in our coming together. It is not the time for solemn silence. We should give the people ample space for silence at those moments indicated in the carefully worked out rubrics of the missal. In the opening rite there is space for silence, for recollection, for coming to a sense of the seriousness of what we are about, for deeper communion with God. The people do need help to come to understand how to use silence and the contribution each of the pauses in the Mass is supposed to make as we move through the celebration. But as the people arrive at their Father's house and first encounter their friends, it is a time for community, for greetings, for celebration.

Some time ago I attended a baptism in an Orthodox church. I marveled at the freedom with which the children played about the church while their elders visited and chatted prior to the service. As it began, the bishop reminded us that children have their own way of honoring their Father by playing in his presence, and little ones often express their praise by sharing the vitality of their lives, crying lustily. We shouldn't make children worship like little adults. Let the children be at home in their Father's house. Then they will grow up being at home with him.

We will speak later about the priest as spiritual father. But the image of the loving papa welcoming his children home for a family gathering is not a bad one for a priest to have as he welcomes his people to the eucharistic liturgy. The basic atmosphere of the Eucharist should be celebration, especially on Sunday, the Lord's Day, the day we celebrate resurrection, hope, final victory. We so much need hope today, since there is so much to depress us. We want this coming together on Sunday to be a time when our hope is renewed because our faith is renewed — something people look forward to and enjoy as one of the high points of the week.

There certainly should come moments of great seriousness. We need to enable the people to enter into the silent places and into the prayer to the Father. There is a time for us, in a sense to leave the people, to talk to the Father. The anaphora is a proclamation, but it is different from the Gospel where we are reading directly to the people. Here we are speaking to the Father, but in a way that is evident to the people. They can hear and see that we are with the Father, by what we are doing and how we are doing it. Our belief is loudly and clearly proclaimed and the people are drawn up into it. *We want really to talk to the Father and mean what we are saying.* This means that the words of the eucharistic prayer have to have become our own. We have to ask ourselves whether we have spent enough personal time with these prayers so that they have in fact become our own. Not so much that we can say them by heart, as that we can pray them from the heart. This is really a key element in our spirituality as priests: that we can pray in this way. Like Christ, with whom we have such a complete identity: "my body . . . my blood," we are called upon to speak to the Father in the name of all as one who has a special bond with him.

Today, much of the emphasis has been on the priest as leader, but we are called priests precisely because we have been ordained to offer sacrifice. There is, of course, a most intimate bond between leadership in the Christian community and leading Eucharist. Rahner goes so far in his theological investigations as to venture the opinion that when lay persons are named to head a particular Christian community (which is happening in some places where there are not sufficient priests for the parishes), these lay persons have the power in virtue of their commission to lead Eucharist, a power that is restricted by present Church discipline. Presiding at the eucharistic celebration is central to our ministry, our leadership, and to our spirituality — these dimensions of our life cannot be separated.

Undoubtedly, there is still much to be done in regard to the theology of the priesthood: the universal priesthood of the Christian wherein all the people offer the sacrifice and the priesthood of the ordained and constituted leader of the Christ-community.

There certainly has been a rich evolution in the theology of the Mass. Today, we are much more profoundly aware of it as the communal celebration. Emphasis is on community. Concelebration has been restored so that all the ordained priests present can exercise the fullness of their priesthood. With this new insight and emphasis, the question comes up: "What if there is no community — should a priest still celebrate Eucharist?" In the past, most devout priests would never think of letting a day slip by without going to the altar. We can remember Mass crypts, side altars, and even the makeshift setups in hotel corridors during conventions. Much of that is happily past. But should a priest ever celebrate alone?

The fact is, of course, a priest never celebrates alone. The Church is a reality. We are always one with the Church and celebrate for all and in the name of all. I think of a hermit who, when he goes to the altar, has before his eyes a globe with the presently most troubled spot in the world facing him as he offers the holy sacrifice.

There is a deep reality here we want to be in touch with. In God all is now. We experience events one after the other, passing along the course of history; but God, as it were, sees them all together in one moment. For him, at the heart of them all, giving meaning to all the rest, is a supreme act of love, for love is the thing most like God and nearest to him. That act of love is the act which Jesus consummated on Calvary's hill. In the supper room, Jesus reached, as it were, into the now of God and brought that act of love forward to be truly present in the new sacramental rite he was then instituting. In going on to institute a priesthood, he gave to others, to every priest who would share in the sacrament he was then instituting, the same power to reach into the now of God and make that supreme act of love actually present again in time. Calvary, the supper, and the Mass are absolutely one in their reality. There is no other sacrifice for the redemption of all. When we bring the sacrifice of Christ into presence, we are able to bring to it our own dispositions, our love, our sacrifices, our prayer of mediation. And these become one with Christ's, to be one with his in the now of God. And thus our part is forever present with the sacrifice of Christ. Whenever Calvary is made present again in time, our offering is there. Indeed, because of this reality, what we bring to each Mass was present on Calvary and in the supper room. Thus it is inconceivable to have a "private" Mass, a Mass apart from the community of the Church, whether or not representatives of the community are present. Their presence brings a due fullness to the sacramental sign and is much to be desired. That is why former legislation made that presence mandatory, at least in the person of an acolyte.

In fact, the community is always represented, for we also are of the community. If, on a particular day, we are free from the call to minister to others, we still can minister to ourselves. Indeed, we need first to minister to ourselves: Love your neighbor — minister to him — as you love yourself. What most truly serves as a sacrament is what most effectively impacts on us in the way a sacrament should. When I am free from the responsibility of actively ministering to others and have only to minister to myself, I should feel free to enter into the sacrament of the Eucharist in whatever way most effectively makes the sacrament with its full meaning present to me at that time, where I am on my personal journey in the Lord. This may mean a very personalized celebration of the Mass. That is fine, so long as we do not distort the sacrament. When we are with others, because the sacrament belongs first to the community, we have to moderate our way of celebration seeking what will best serve the community assembled. But when we ourselves are the whole community being ministered to, we are the Church present, and as minister we gear the celebration to our particular needs.

The solitary Mass is probably not the great concern of most priests. Their concern lies in the need to celebrate the Mass well when it needs to be celebrated repeatedly for the community. I am sure some, as they have been reading through this chapter, have thought to themselves: "All this is wonderful in theory, but in practice. . . . When you have to do it two, three, four, five times on a Sunday morning?" It is difficult, if not nearly impossible, to truly celebrate again and again on demand. Welcoming and cultivating the full support of the various ministers can be an immense help. But it is only by deep prayer — that particular prayer which leaves us in constant contact with the Source, the Divine Creative Energy at the center of our being — that we will be able to celebrate again and again in a meaningful and effective way. We cannot do it out of our own limited resources. We can do it out of the infinite love that Christ has for his Father and for his people, that love which is truly within us and is ours to use. It has been given to us as Gift. This Love, the Holy Spirit, can make us so aware of the Reality of what we are doing, can so fill us with love for the people we are making this Reality present to, so energize us that we can in truth celebrate.

Nonetheless, maybe it is time to have the courage to innovate a bit on the way we have been doing things and seek possibilities of greater quality by relieving the priest from some of the oppressive quantity. Rescheduling can be of some help, no doubt. In many places in the world, Christian people have learned to celebrate Sunday with a Liturgy of the Word and Communion service without the benefit of a priest on a regular basis. Why would it not be possible in an understaffed parish to allow lay persons to lead some services such as these and limit the priest to the one or two Masses he can effectively celebrate? The people would have the choice and could be encouraged to choose Mass at least from time to time. Another possibility would be to allow the people the option of attending this Eucharist some other day in place of Sunday, especially if they have to work on Sunday and to take their day of rest some other day of the week. Maybe such changes are not possible yet. But don't be too quick to say so or feel that the initiative for such changes always has to come from above. The pastor has been given a mission, a pastoral office in regard to his parish, and should use all the creativity he reasonably can to improve the quality of his service and the well-being of his people. Our attitude in serving should be not that we can do only what we are told but that we are free to do everything we have not been forbidden. And we can do even the forbidden when there is a sufficient reason to do so. *Epieikeia* has always been a respected part of our tradition at least in theory — perhaps more in practice in the East than in the West.

We want to seek what is best for our people creatively in the way of providing Masses and in the way we celebrate them. We need to call them forth to the fullest possible participation in bringing this about. But we do want to be prudently clear that our creativity is coming out of the Source, the Divine Creative Love who dwells in us all, who brings us forth in his love, and who teaches us all things, calling to mind whatever Jesus has taught us. We don't want to be creative or different just to attract attention to ourselves, or to enhance our reputation, or to seek novelty for novelty's sake. All is in service.

It's the Mass that matters — the celebration of the Eucharist. Not with any understanding that if the priest offers Mass it is enough. Not precisely that the celebration of the Eucharist is the priest's most important activity. The fact is that the Mass is absolutely the central thing, the event that matters. It is the ultimate act of love that makes all the difference in our human existence. When it gets down to it, almost everything we can do as priests can also be done by duly constituted lay persons except lead the Eucharist, making Calvary present and applying its healing in the special way that it is applied in the sacrament of reconciliation. We will more effectively create the sacramental reality of reconciliation the more we are aware that it flows from the Mass-Calvary, and it actually flows in and through us as being empowered by the experience of our mediatorial role at the altar. Others can prepare the people for Eucharist through catechesis and baptism and share out the fruit of the Mass through Communion. The priest makes it present, essentially forming Christian community, calling it forth from the side of Christ, cleansed in his blood to be nourished by his body and blood. If the Mass, in all the levels of its reality, is central in my life as a priest and all that I do flows from it, I will necessarily be a good priest.

Our function of leadership in the person of Christ reaches its apex in this celebration just as it did for Christ on Calvary, one with the whole of the paschal mystery of death, resurrection, and ascension. We will be able to lead as we want, as a Christ-person, only if we have truly died to our false self so that our true Christ-self can express itself unhindered. This Christ-self is not separate from true humanity. Jesus sweat blood, knew every human emotion, every human pain. But he also knew who he was, what he was about, and had the ultimate freedom to cut through all the turmoil, emotion, and pain to say a complete and unconditional "yes" to the Father even as he embraced in totally compassionate love — "Father, forgive them; for they know not what they do" (Luke 23:34) — each and all of his sisters and brothers. When we can lead into a true experience of this all-embracing, all-healing love, we are most truly who we are as men who have been ordained into the priestly role within the People of God who are Christ. To understand, we not only must apply our minds to theology, we must go beyond and open ourselves to the understanding and sapiential experience that comes from the activity of the gifts of the Holy Spirit. We want to know as Paul knew: "I know in whom I believe"; and to live in response to that, in our freedom to embrace the reality that we are to the Father in the Son in our whole life stance. This we will be able to do only if we do go into our room and pray to the Father in secret, letting our consciousness be molded and formed by Christ.

5

Praying with the Church

The "official" prayer of the Church — the divine office, or the breviary — is certainly not the most important thing in the life of a priest, not even in the life of the monastic priest, even though the Benedictine rule says "nothing is to be preferred to the Work of God." But it is a challenge for each one of us. The prayer of the hours is not the most important thing, but it does make a big difference in our lives and in the life of the Church if we are faithful to it.

Sacred reading is an important element in Christian life: faith comes from the word of the Lord. In practice we need *three kinds of sacred reading* — not always clearly or completely distinguished in our practice. Nonetheless, it is good for us to be aware of our diverse needs. I have already spoken about this, but let me return to it a bit here because it is, I think, so essential to our keeping alive and effective as priests. It is also relevant to a significant part of the daily office.

First of all, we need *sacred study*, that is, reading geared to the intellect, to knowing and understanding the revelation and everything else in the light of the revelation. We are to love the Lord our God with our whole mind. We want to stretch our edges and ever seek a deeper and fuller knowledge of the word of the Lord, what he has revealed to us. Faith seeks understanding so that it can be effectively present in our lives. If this dimension of Christian life is important to all men and women of faith, it is particularly important to us who are, so to speak, professionals in the faith. It is important that we keep up-to-date in our field.

We need to keep up not only with the changes in Church law — and that is difficult enough — but with the development of doctrine, the new insights that respond to the needs of our times and make the age-old teaching relevant, be able to speak effectively to our people today. We need to be current with normal theology's responses to new ethical questions and the ramifications of the new contributions from the behavioral sciences. We cannot expect the Holy Spirit to work today through yesterday's theology. If our ministry is going to be effective, it has to be up-to-date.

This is not easy to achieve. Many dioceses and deaneries do provide study days. These are a help, although it has always been difficult for me to see how a priest or religious can be expected to keep producing at full speed and to keep up-to-date without ever having a sabbatical. If other teaching fields (where the demands are so much less) see this as imperative, it seems to me it would be very important to build a sabbatical program into sacred ministry — and, of course, cultivate in ourselves an appreciation and desire for such opportunities. In dioceses where sabbaticals are offered, relatively few men have actually availed themselves of them. In any case, we each need to do what we can. We need to chisel out a couple of hours a week, at least, for some hard study: the encyclicals, the bishops' pastorals, the documents of Vatican II (if they are not already fully assimilated) for starters. The challenge of fine theological minds like Rahner, Dulles, and even a Hans Küng can add a crispness to our understanding of what we do hold, and make our preaching, teaching, and ministry more alive and effective. If we are not up-to-date in our moral theology, we could be hurting the people we want to help by forming in them a false conscience. Whether it be on the side of strictness or laxity, it can impede their growth and even imperil their immortal well-being. Our responsibility is great. We have to do what we can. I think we would be the first to advise a doctor that he had a serious moral obligation to lighten his case load if that is necessary in order to give himself the time he needs to do the study that will keep him from hurting his patients. Physician, heal thyself.

It is not enough to know, obviously. We need to live up to the insight that is given us. Thus, besides the study or sacred reading that renews our minds we also need that faith sharing or reading which will renew our wills. We need enough *motivational reading* to support us in being a complete "yes" to all that God makes known to us. This reading can be quite general, fostering our devotion to our divine Master, supporting our basic wholeheartedness. Or it can be quite specific, responding to a need for renewal in a particular area: The celebration of the Eucharist just isn't all it should be for me, so I turn to a good book on the Mass, for instance, and seek further insight and motivation to be more with it.

Finally, there is a kind of sacred reading that is not directly geared toward enlightening the mind or moving the will but rather is the space for an encounter with God. It seeks to go beyond the words to the experience of God. This is the traditional *lectio divina*. We just want God to reveal himself to us, make himself present through his word. And if he does that in the first word we read, we abide there, for we have what we want. If he does not, we just let the words wash over us, purifying, increasing our desire, until he whom we seek is found, as he has promised.

All three kinds of sacred reading are found within the office. At particular moments we will be more conscious of one, seek one more than the others. Most fundamentally though the office is *lectio*, it is a reading that seeks to enter into immediate experiential contact with God. That is the consummation of prayer, and the office is prayer, the prayer of the Church. So we should never hesitate to lay our breviary aside or leave off saying the words if the Lord draws us into a deeper experience of himself. It will be in that more intimate embrace that we will draw the People of God most closely to the Lord and obtain for them most effectively the blessings they need.

This particular chapter of our book is more in the nature of the second kind of sacred reading: motivational — though some of the first kind, informational, will be here. If at some point the Lord comes through — well, drop the book and be with him. That holds for the whole book. At any time we may set out with primarily one kind of reading in mind, aware perhaps of a particular need. And the Lord may respond in another way. He knows what is best for us, what we really need at the moment. I can remember when I was a theology student, one day struggling over a bit of Rahner, chewing on just about every word in every sentence of his dense prose. It was an article about Christology in a world evolving view. Then suddenly it all came together. It was perhaps something like the vision that Gregory describes Benedict having: seeing the whole creation under a single ray of light. It certainly transformed not only my whole outlook on life but my whole sense of God, his presence, and his love. The Lord is the master of his gifts.

The Constitution on the Sacred Liturgy of the Second Vatican Council devotes only a few paragraphs to the theology of the divine office. Much of Chapter 4 is devoted to more practical considerations, though these are well connected with the theological realities and thus enhance our understanding. Primarily the liturgy of the hours is seen as Christ in and through his Church ceaselessly praising his Father and interceding for the entire world.

It certainly can help us to realize just what is really

going on when we pray the office. We are so painfully aware of our own weaknesses and oftentimes distracted state as pray-ers that it is difficult for us to place great value in what is being done. What is helpful for us to know is that when we pray the office, yes, we pray; but another also prays, the Lord, and his Spirit, for he always prays in the Spirit. The words of our lips have a divine efficacy because we have given them to the God-man. Jesus now prays these words, and he prays them as they ought to be prayed. Our poverty and misery as pray-ers are swallowed up in his prayer.

It is the whole Christ who prays — the whole Body of Christ, the whole Church. I think it is important for us to realize this for two reasons. First of all, the Church needs prayer. Who can doubt that? Just a momentary glance around the world, beginning with our own immediate community, can overwhelm us with the fact of that need. Prayer is the one thing we can do about everything. So we give our mouths and our minds as best we can to the Church and let the People of God pray now through us. This realization is where we experience and are confirmed in the reality of our mediatorial role. This seems to me to be particularly important today when our personal meaning as priest is being battered on every side. We do, of course, exercise our mediation supremely in the Mass, very significantly in the sacraments, but perhaps singularly in the office, where no other ministry is involved. Here we are mediators, or the whole thing makes little sense. If all I were concerned about was prayer, I certainly would not burden myself with these words and forms. But I take the words and forms given me by the Church so that in some very existential and palpable way the Church prays through me through the words of my lips and the sentiments of my heart — for integrity requires that in some way we seek to bring our hearts into conformity with what our lips are saying.

As we give our lips to the Church it is not just the community of the faithful spread across the globe today who pray through us. It is the Church that has gone before. Mary and Joseph pray again the psalms, as does David, their author. All the saints, our own special patrons, the great ones and the unknown ones, all pray now with our lips. Sometimes it can be helpful to reflect specifically on this and even be aware of a particular one praying with us, letting such a one help form the sentiments of our hearts. We can pray the psalms with Mary, hearing them as she would hear them, praying them as she would pray them. The same, of course, for our divine Master, or his foster father, Joseph, or a priest close to us in life and ministry: John Vianney, John Bosco, John Newman, or any other. They are all with us in the prayer of the Church, for they, like ourselves, are the Church.

Praise does not come easily to us. Much of our life experience, especially for us men, rather encourages us to be competitive, to try to knock the other down and keep him down so that we can get ahead, rather than to praise and affirm. We don't even readily praise ourselves. We experience too much hollowness — besides, that wouldn't be humble and we want people to at least think we are humble if nothing else.

Our initial experience in life is one of hollowness and need. We come forth from the womb needing everything. And we yowl for what we need: warmth, stroking, food, nurture of every kind, all sorts of things. As our consciousness grows we become quite aware of those who provide these things we need and want. These people become very significant in our lives. We need to please them to keep on getting what we need and want.

An unfortunate thing begins to happen at this point. The people, usually our parents, who provide for us in our first helplessness, are very like God and sacraments of his wholly gratuitous love. Such love affirms our essential worth, tells us that we do not have to earn love, that we are lovable in our very selves. But usually, these significant persons begin to trade on that love and make demands in the name of that love: Mama won't love Johnny if he doesn't eat his spinach — Daddy won't love Sue if she doesn't put away her dolls or get a gold star in school.

And on and on. Then we begin to identify with a false self, one made up of what we have, what people think of us, and what we can do. We see this in the way most men on introducing themselves immediately tell us what they do. It is part of their identity. This is one of the reasons it is so difficult for men to retire. If for forty years I have been "Joe Jones — I work at Sperry's" or "Bill Rogers — I teach at the university" and then I am suddenly just "Joe Jones" or "Bill Rogers" I have suffered a severe diminishment. A sense of self is lost. (We could each ask ourselves: "When I introduce myself, how quickly do I add what I am doing, the role I am filling, or some acquired title? How much have I brought into the false self?")

We see something of this false self among our people in their religious practice — and it is why some have found renewal so difficult. For all too many people God is the significant one out there whom they have to please to get the eternal goodies. And that is the sum total of their religious life: What they have to do to keep in God's good graces to get what they want here and hereafter. Before the renewal this seemed fairly easy. People were told that if they went to Mass on Sunday and didn't eat meat on Friday they had it made. But with the renewal it isn't so simple. Friday abstinence has for the most part gone by the boards and Sunday Mass is not so rigorously demanded. But all these other requirements are being thrown at us: social justice, care for the poor and oppressed, disarmament, desegregation. . . . How are we to be sure we have it made with God? Thanks be to God, we can't be so sure. We are thrown into a living relationship.

The false self that seeks to mask our hollowness is a very fragile self. We can so easily lose things; lose other people's good offices; lose our ability to do and achieve. So we become very defensive and competitive. What we need, of course, is a transformation of consciousness so that we do not identify ourselves with a false self but come to know our true self, come to know that we are not hollow but that at that center of our being is an all-loving, ever-creating God, who totally loves us, completely, gratuitously, makes us in his very own image and promises to give us whatever we ask of him: "Ask and you shall receive." With such affirmation we need not worry about what others think of us. With such a Source within us we need not depend on what we have. If we are concerned about our doings, it is only because that is the way we can express our love in return.

When we are in secure possession of our own magnificence, when we know we are the infinitely loved children of God, then we can freely acknowledge and rejoice in the magnificence of others. Our hearts overflow with gratitude and praise of the Source of all this and in praise of all that he has done.

Humanly speaking, this is not always easy. We see — too readily and in some cases perhaps a bit too self-righteously — the flaws in others and in the creation. We see the holes and miss the doughnut; we see the superficial absence of goodness and miss the underlying goodness. For just as there can be no hole without the doughnut, there can be no evil without some good from which it detracts. The evil still pains us. It can hurt us deeply. But when we have experienced something of the goodness of God himself through deep prayer, we see deeply enough to know that he does have everything under control.

We have an exceptionally beautiful brother in our community. His whole life is one of praise. He quietly praises God for everything, no matter how disastrous things seem. His life is built on faith, on the word of the Lord: "We know that God makes all things work together for the good of those who love him" (Romans 8:28); "For my thoughts are not your thoughts, / neither are your ways my ways, says the LORD. / For as the heavens are higher than the earth, / so are my ways higher than your ways / and my thoughts than your thoughts" (Isaiah 55:8-9).

It is only when this reality has become real for us that the outpourings of praise we find in the liturgy of the hours can come from the depths of our own hearts. In the meantime we may have to be for the most part but the lips of those others in the Body who know this and pray that more and more our own hearts will be formed to that knowledge of his glory that perfects praise.

This is part of the role of the hours in our lives, and one that we need: that our hearts will be formed according to the heart of Christ. The constant repetition of these prayers and sentiments that he prayed, that speak of him and speak to him, and he speaks in us, will gradually form our own hearts in their likeness. The office is a school of prayer. We do not know how to pray as we ought, but in it the Spirit prays in us and teaches us how to pray. If some of the sentiments of the hours are strange to us, not really what we would spontaneously pray of ourselves, we should not be surprised. We are all beginners in this. We have much to learn. The deeper meanings will gradually reveal themselves.

There are many ways in which we can actually go about praying the office. The most obvious is, to express it in the traditional way, to bring the mind into harmony with the voice. We seek to identify with the sentiments of the prayers and make them our own. This can give expression to feelings that are already very present. Or awaken sentiments long dormant. Or teach us new ways of relating to the Lord. I have already mentioned an alternate possibility: listening to the words through the ears of another — Jesus, Mary, one of the saints, or another member of the Church — and seeking to be in tune with the sentiments they would have. The present experience of the Church and our place within it can also strongly color our perception and expression.

Too much effort along these lines can be tiring. Our Lord said: "Come to me, all who labor and are heavy laden, and I will give you rest" (Matthew 11:28). Prayer should be refreshing. There are simpler ways to pray the office. We might just latch on to one of the sentiments expressed and simply abide peacefully in it before the Lord as our lips or minds go on with the words given to us.

Even more simply, the words as a whole might just be background music, supplying the space wherein we abide simply and lovingly with the Lord, letting his love renew and refresh us. We are the Church to the Lord more by the sentiment or movement of our heart than by any of the words we might say or thoughts we might conceive. The heart is at the heart of the matter.

Remember always that the office is an office of prayer. All of it is at the service of prayer. If then during our praying it we are drawn into a deeper, more silent prayer, let us not hesitate to let go of the texts or the words, and be with the Lord in the silence. We are fulfilling our responsibility to pray for, with, and in the Church.

Again, at times we might better pray if, instead of hastening through all the day's texts, we prayed one of the psalms or prayers slowly and let it be more fully expressed in us. If the breviary sends us hither and thither, looking for this piece and that, and we find all of this more distracting than helpful, we should not hesitate to simplify the office and stay more prayerfully with the essential parts or the common, rather than go chasing after elusive antiphons or versicles. The thing is to pray, to be to God in praise and supplication.

We are urged to pray the hours at their appropriate times: morning and evening, some time during the day, and when retiring. If we are truly impeded, especially if we are impeded by other ministries of prayer at a particular time, we can offer what we are doing as our prayer to sanctify that period. It does not make much sense at the end of a long, full day to begin to pray morning prayers. That is obvious. It is equally obvious that we should not let our life be habitually so pushed around that we cannot have time with the Lord morning and evening and in between — at least the few minutes it takes to pray the hours. The priest is a man of prayer — who would not define him so? And a man of prayer should frequently be at prayer. The office affords us a supportive structure to do that.

The Constitution on the Sacred Liturgy urges even diocesan priests to pray some of the office in common. Not easy! But possible and maybe a great blessing for rectory life and for the community that is commonly served. Not too long ago I was at dinner in the home of a wealthy Catholic family. As the meal came to an end the youngest son (they had nine children around the table) took a big humidor from the sideboard and approached the table. I wondered if they were going to offer the guests — another priest, my mother, and myself — cigars. When the box was opened, it revealed a large collection of rosaries. The little fellow made the rounds of the table and each took a rosary. We then prayed the family rosary. When the priests of the parish are gathered for any meal, could they not invite their guests to join them at the end in praying the appropriate hour? I suspect most guests would be delighted. When they are alone, of course, the priests would be completely free to do this — provided they prudently leave some space in their planning so as not to have to rush through meals and be off to appointments.

The Constitution on the Sacred Liturgy also encourages the laity to take up the office as their prayer and suggests that pastors make some provisions for this. In England I found morning and evening prayer quite frequent in Anglican parishes, less frequent among Roman Catholics but common enough. In the United States I find the rosary more common. Maybe some reeducation is needed here. If some of the faithful can gather for the rosary before or after Mass, they probably could be introduced to the idea of praying the office with their pastor. This is being explored in more parishes with surprising results. Perhaps a simplified breviary would serve better here. One publishing company, Doubleday, has put out an inexpensive paperback called *Prayertimes: Morning — Midday — Evening Prayer*, which could serve well.

If we schedule a time for praying the office in church, we may well find ourselves at times praying it alone. Nonetheless, much is still gained. Such a schedule provides a certain support for our own prayer, a certain accountability — if we are not going to be able to make it, we will have to render some account to those who might come. Moreover, it lets the people know that their priest is praying for them. It can be a very consoling bit of knowledge, especially to those who are troubled or sick, to know at certain times the pastor is in the parish church praying for them, to know that they can unite their prayer at that time with his. Every parishioner will know that in times of stress and need they can go to the church at the appointed time and find someone to pray with them; they can find their pastor there to get counsel and comfort from him after prayer. If periods of meditation or Centering Prayer can be added to the office, this could be an even richer spiritual oasis available on life's journey. And it would support the priest in his own fidelity to this contemplative prayer that he also needs. If we are wise, we will build into our ministry as much as possible the supports we need and the spaces of prayer.

In regard to the liturgy of the hours I would suggest you keep this in mind about rigidity and flexibility. *Rigidity*: never omit it; *flexibility*: for any good reason adjust it. Shorten it, if you have to, to a psalm you can say by heart and a brief prayer; or if you can't even do that, then just a conscious offering up of what you are doing as your prayer and through you the prayer of the Church for that hour. Shorten it if necessary, lengthen it if you want to, but never omit it. Let all the hours of your life be holy, sanctified in some way by prayer. Let them all ascend to God as the prayer of the Church for the Church, which has such need of our prayer and has commissioned us to be men of prayer.

6

As One
Who Serves

●

"To have lived is not enough, we have to talk about it," says Samuel Bechett. And that is what we do. We get together and talk about what we are doing, what's going on. Sometimes it sounds as if we are trying to top one another, but it is always a genuine sharing. These sharings are witness stories and they have a power in them. They give us the opportunity to acknowledge the Lord working through us. They also allow the listener to identify with the story and plug into its energy: an energy that at times can give new life to what we are about — new life to our work, to our ministry.

This word, "ministry," is applicable not only to what we do but also to what the faithful do with us in our common sacred mission. It is a shared labor. And in the sharing we experience both agony and ecstasy. Agony, when everyone seems to be telling us what to do, how to do it, and that what we are doing isn't right or good enough, and yet asking even more of us. And, of course, it isn't just the good people who are working with us who do this. There are the endless number of packages and letters. Each day the mail seems to bring yet another request, another program, another letter to be read. Where I come from they call it the "funnel syndrome" — all this material being funneled into us for immediate action. Where are we to find all the time and energy for this? And yet, wonder of wonders, we do. We get it all done and for the most part well done.

On the other side is the ecstasy: having all these co-laborers. Coresponsibility: that is where the energy comes from to get it all done. In the past we were expected to fulfill all the responsibilities of ministry by ourselves; it was the priest's job. He ministered and the people were ministered unto. Now we are blessed with many coworkers, many helpers who are beginning to truly realize that this is their parish, their school, their apostolate. . . . With such realization comes an ever greater commitment on their part to walk all the way with us in serving the People of God.

The new experience of shared responsibility can also have its moments of agony. I have come to believe that we do not need to take on any special penances in this age of shared responsibility. For there is no greater form of mortification, of dying to self in order to live to others, than conducting or attending meetings with a spirit of openness and collegiality. If we are conducting the meeting, we need to be alert to all that is expressed and patiently lead the group toward consensus. If we are attending a meeting, we always experience the need to be patient with the pace of things. "Why can't others grasp this as quickly as I do? It is so obvious (to me)." Meetings are truly the penance of our age. They are a very necessary part of our lives, for if we are truly sharing in the priesthood of Christ as Head, then there must be meetings where we communicate with the members of Christ in order to coordinate the activity of the whole priestly body, ordained and nonordained.

We have identified the essence of our ordained priesthood to lie in being sacraments of Christ the Head forming community within the Church, the sacrament of saving unity. If we lose sight of this, we are in danger of seeing our ministry in too functional a role; our ministry is seen as what we do and nothing more. That is not the reality. We are a person-symbol, a sacrament of Christ the Head. It is only when we have a sure grasp of who we are that we can speak about what we do, without losing the profound significance that is inherent in all that we do as priests. Our being and our doing must be intimately one if we are to be truly effective as priests. Herein lies the source of our power in ministry.

The title of this chapter seeks to highlight the fact that our ministry is service. We do not seek power for ourselves but to empower others, to call them forth more powerfully to the fullness of life in Christ to which they are called. Like Jesus we always come to ministry "as one who serves." I have always resonated to that statement of Lacordaire which was so popular when I was in the seminary:

> To live in the midst of the world
> without wishing its pleasures,
> to be a member of every family
> yet belonging to none,
> to share all sufferings,
> to penetrate all secrets,
> to heal all wounds,
> to go from men [and women] to God
> and offer him their prayers,
> to return from God to men [and women],
> to bring pardon and joy.
> My God, what a life!
> And it is yours,
> O priest of Jesus Christ.

It is in a ministry of service that we seek to employ our many and varied gifts, all of which flow from the same life-giving source. "Now there are varieties of gifts, but the same Spirit; and there are varieties of service, but the same Lord; and there are varieties of working, but it is the same God who inspires them all in every one. To each is given the manifestation of the Spirit for the common good" (1 Corinthians 12:4-7).

Using our gifts in a ministry of service, we priests work out our own salvation and share in the redemptive work of our Lord Jesus. "Every priest will find in his very vocation and ministry the deep motivation for living his entire life in oneness and strength of Spirit. Called like the rest of those who have been baptized to become a true image of Christ (Rom 8:29), the priest, like the apostles, shares besides in a special way companionship with Christ and his mission. . . . In the priestly life there can be no dichotomy between love for Christ and zeal for souls" (National Conference of Catholic Bishops).

There are times when we do wonder what makes the difference in what we are doing. So much of our time and energy seem to be absorbed by the details of life, in tending to everyday human doings. We are inclined to think it should be otherwise. When my brother was in the military, I visited him at his base in the South. While I was there, we decided to visit a nearby monastery. My brother's new wife was with us and I very much wanted her to be impressed — which is not an uncommon fault of priestly brothers-in-law. I told her about the tremendous dedication of the monks to the spiritual life, saying, "They are not caught up in all the distractions of the world like we are." When we arrived at the abbey, we went into the bookstore. We had not browsed very long before the brother tending the shop sort of shepherded me off into a corner. In a whisper that it would have been impossible for my sister-in-law to not hear, he began a long lament about all the activities the monks were getting involved in. They were distracting this good man from truly giving his time and attention wholly to the Lord. As I looked over his shoulder I could see my sister-in-law smiling mischievously. It was a good lesson for me. Every human vocation, even that of the Son of Man and that of his chosen contemplatives, has had to work itself out within the context of an ordinary human life with all its distractions.

But what really makes the difference? I don't think it is what we do, nor the degree of success or failure we encounter. What makes the difference is the vision and the heart we put into what we do, whether it be something sublime, a thing of transcendent faith, or a humble human service, a homey response to basic human needs. Our vision, our love, the intention we want to bring to all that we do, little or great, is the honest desire to further the mission of Christ and of his Church. We want to be instruments of God's love acting in the here-and-now situation, stirring up and activating the divine love present in those whom we serve, so that it might leaven their actions, situations, and institutions. "Thy kingdom come" is our constant prayer; even while we seek to remember that already "the kingdom of God is within." The loving wisdom that motivates us is that the presence of the kingdom be recognized by all and become effective in the lives of all, creating its likeness in our society and in the whole human family.

How do we go about assuring that this loving vision remains present in our ministry of service so that we will make a difference?

A number of years ago, when I was active in the family life ministry and preparing for the 1980 Year of the Family, I attended a presentation by a Father William McNulty. That presentation inspired me to write on the renewal of leadership in the Church. Through the years this has evolved into a "process of ministry." No, this is not another program, something more to do. I don't have time for that, nor do you. It is rather a way of looking at things, an overview that has enabled me to get a better grip on what I am actually doing and to keep my vision clear. It has helped me to remain more fully grounded in faith and keep to the journey as a disciple of Jesus Christ, aware of the kingdom of God within and working for the establishment of the kingdom of God in this world of ours.

As I have conceived of it, there are four aspects or elements. They are:

1. An Awareness That Understands — The Person

Recall the story of Martha and Mary (Luke 10:38-42). Martha served Jesus while Mary ministered to him. Martha served Jesus with a lot of energy and planning. Mary ministered to Jesus by being present to him. From the story it is evident that at that particular moment Jesus wanted someone to be present to him. Even though both of the women knew Jesus quite well and knew what they usually did when he came to their home, on this particular occasion Mary perceived that it was not to be business as usual. Jesus was in another space. Mary responded to Jesus in this different space. This is the first aspect of effective ministry: an awareness that understands.

This awareness that understands involves the total person of the minister — all levels. To be good ministers it is necessary for us to be aware of the everyday reality, of the way things usually function. We need to be aware of ourselves with our strengths and weaknesses, our style of ministry and the effect we have on others. We need to be aware of our gifts, the gifts we bring to ministry. How do we respond to success — and to failure? Are we more concerned about content or medium? An awareness that understands demands self-knowledge and at the same time self-acceptance of our own uniqueness.

We need to know the place of our ministry in the overall life of those to whom we minister and to the Church: the parish or school, the diocese, the larger Church. We are sons of God, made in his image, anointed and blessed by his signs of love, the sacraments. We are members of his Body, the Church. As partakers of his life, our daily lives take on a new dimension. And this new dimension is not just something superimposed by laws, prayers, activities, or ordination. It flows from the inner reality of our being, from a Source that is within us. Our special vocation calls us to be aware of God's presence in ourselves, to be aware of his presence in our relationships with others, to be aware of his presence in the message we deliver and in the programs we facilitate, to be aware of his presence in the plowing, planting, and harvesting of our ministry. Our presence is more than ourselves: he is present when we are truly present.

He is also present when others present themselves to us. All that we have said about what we need to be aware of in regard to ourselves is applicable to the persons to whom we minister. We need to take the time to know them, to know their story, their strengths, their weaknesses, their style, the effect they have on others, their reactions, their calling and their commitment to that calling, their gifts, their way of measuring their successes and their failures, and their openness to the ideas that we might present to them. Our response has to be in accord with where the person is at the moment. Sometimes when people come to us, we need to spend most of the time creating the peace that will encourage them to open up. Other times they are ready, thus it is time to plant some seed. And other times when they come, it is a time to listen to their story, for they are reaping the harvest of the plowing and planting that has gone before.

2. A Caring That Enables — Empowerment

Recall now the story of the woman at the well (John 4:7-42). Jesus wanted a drink. The occasion becomes one of deeper communication and conversation. An acceptance and freeing took place, and the woman was empowered to tell her life story. A bond grew between them and yet Jesus did not try to hang on to her or let her hang on to him. Rather he empowered her to tell her story to the people in her community and draw them to him. This is the second aspect of ministry: a caring that enables.

A caring that enables is a genuine reaching out, an

encounter, an affirmation of another and a healing. Our reaching out is to be to all, as is Jesus', not just to some. This reaching out confronts us with the reality that we, too, need healing and affirmation. Ministry is a two-way street, a giving and a receiving, for as we give life we become more filled with life. Caring that enables is not simply "doing good." It is not simply "being of service." Caring is a process of creation, not a process of dependence. When we are aware of the presence of God in another, our caring enables the other to see one's own worth, one's potential, one's ability to care for oneself, one's ability to reach out and help others. As Henri Nouwen put it: "To care is the human capacity to listen to the other without asking what advantage that has for me; to reach out a hand without expecting anything in return; to give without condition and to receive with simple thankfulness. To care is therefore to be present to the other."

This is a caring that enables others to take ownership of their own lives. We do not want to control anyone. We want to help others take responsibility for themselves. We try to make it possible for them to search themselves, examine their motives, and untangle their feelings. This could be a lively and creative activity for ourselves as well as for them on the journey toward maturity. It is not a question of poking into other people's lives, but being present when they need us. We help them reaffirm their own identities. We help them lower their defenses and see the truth about themselves that will free them to grow. We encourage and support them to continue on the journey.

This does not require a great deal of time. However, it does require that time be used well. We need to develop a deep commitment to what we are about and avoid any superficial approach to others. Our presence is a healing presence because we accept others on their own terms and encourage them to take their own lives seriously, to trust in their own special vocation, their own special calling. In doing this we empower them to do the same for others. We give them what time and care they need and then we send them on their way. I have always been amazed, meditating on our Lord's life, on how many times he sent people away after ministering to them. Many times people wanted to stay with him, yet he sent them home. He cut them loose. He trusted that the Spirit would be in them to help them to go ahead on their own and minister to others.

3. Hospitality That Ministers — The Leadership

Walk with the disciples on their way to Emmaus (Luke 24:13-53). They were part of Jesus' leadership group. They were dedicated, they were together, and they thought they knew what their mission was. Now they were passing through a period of great trial. Doubts gripped their hearts. Jesus came along. He stayed with them only long enough to get them through their trial and then he left them. They were ready to return to Jerusalem to proclaim the Good News. This is the third dimension of ministry: hospitality that ministers.

For a service that ministers there needs to be the virtue of hospitality. We must create an environment that encourages mutual sharing and trust. In hospitality there exists a tension between compulsiveness and compassion. In trying to discern which of the two is operative in the hospitality we are offering we need to answer the question: "How important is it to me that the hospitality I am offering be relevant, spectacular, or powerful?" If what we are doing has to be relevant, it is difficult for us simply to be present. If the goal is to make ourselves more powerful, it is impossible for us to be present to the other and to what really is. Maybe the word powerful is not right. Maybe it is a question of having to control, to be well-thought of, and to be right. When these become the primary motives of the hospitality we offer, then it is very difficult to say that the service that follows is one that truly ministers. We know we are into compulsive ministry and hospitality when our tendency is to seek

113

quick solutions. We want to handle the situation without giving it and the people involved the time they deserve. This attitude turns us into rulers, controllers, and manipulators and it prevents real community from taking place.

Service without hospitality creates impatient people, people who do not want to suffer and share others' burdens. Service without hospitality creates distance and leads to hostility. Service without hospitality is often offending rather than liberating, and it is all too often refused by those who need it.

Service with hospitality leads to compassion. As we interact and encourage one another we are aware of the "wholesomeness" of our activity. Service is not just providing solutions or fulfilling needs, but affirming the other. This takes a little extra time. We need to treat others as persons, sensitive to their needs, concerned with the totality of their existence. Their expectation is that they will be responded to as persons. We bring our wholeness to ministry, to help our peers discover their wholeness. They take us into their lives — we cannot remain outside.

A hospitality that serves out of compassion offers ministry; the person is truly ministered to. In the story of Jesus with his disciples at Emmaus, the disciples had already experienced together an awareness that understands because they were his disciples; they had been shown the caring that enabled them to take ownership of what was expected of them. But they now had some doubts. They needed to experience the hospitality of the Lord in order to be ministered to. They were not too sure what was the basis of what they were about. Jesus took the time to walk with them, sit with them, break bread with them, and explain the Good News to them so that they might continue their journey to a deeper level.

Is this not our task with our various staffs, our faculties, with our communities? Sometimes we forget that we, the leaders, need to minister to one another. There is so much to be done that it is easy to forget this. We are, after all, "wounded healers."

4. Structures That Facilitate — Organization

Read again that passage from Saint Paul's letter to the Corinthians where we hear that beautiful image of Christ the Body of which each one of us is a part (1 Corinthians 12:27-31). We have a need of one another within a structure, which is the Body of Christ. There is a structure here. Now reflect on the Gospel passage where the mother of James and John approaches Jesus asking for an important position for her sons in the Lord's kingdom, the structure (Matthew 20:20-28). Not only was Jesus unable to promise her anything in this regard but the two men's ambition expressed by their mother created dissension among the disciples. No one can minister on his own or for his own glory and advantage. We are part of a whole, a body, a structure, that calls forth an interdependence on one another. What we do affects the whole body structure, and what the structure does affects us. The fourth element in our ministry is structures that facilitate.

In order for us to consistently allow awareness to understand, caring to enable, and hospitality to minister, there must be a structure to create the proper environment and climate that will facilitate all of this. The renewal of each individual person is very essential. Ministering to the individual is the purpose of our call. But, at the same time, there is a need constantly to renew the structures so that this ministry may continue. We need to be aware of the value of structures and the role of those involved in making them operate so that they can support and contribute. Through this awareness we come to a greater understanding of the role we play in the overall picture. There is need to care about structure, but to care about it in such a way that people will be enabled by it and not imprisoned. There is a need to be of service to structure so that the structure can minister to us and to others, allowing us to go deeper into the mystery of Church, which is symbolized by the institutional structure. We minister to organization and structure because is the place where people meet and grow. Structures can be set up in such a way so that they are very bureaucratic with great emphasis on authority. But that need not be the case. Structures can be supportive and even therapeutic, wholly ordered to helping individuals. They can be participative, allowing the community to exercise authority within them. They can be collaborative, where the numbers share in the decision making in the context of dialogue. In reality, all structure should possess something of each of these elements: supportive, therapeutic, participative, and collaborative.

The important thing for us to remember is that structures need to be ministered to so that they can facilitate true ministry. This calls for discernment as to what needs to be done, what needs to be changed in planning, scheduling, and goal orientation. It is almost diabolical how certain patterns and customs can establish themselves and subtly become obstacles to the very ministry that the structures are meant to foster and to the spiritual well-being of those serving the structures or working within them.

These then are four elements of ministry I try to keep an eye on in my service of and for the kingdom: an awareness that understands, a caring that enables, a hospitality that ministers, and structures that facilitate.

There are other approaches, complementary one to another. I like the approach of Father John Shea. He speaks about ministry in terms of being present: lingering with the person, event, or members of the institution. For him, this lingering, this ministerial presence, has three dimensions:

First, we want to be with the people we minister to in their *actual* situation. This means that we actually know where they are at, what they are actually going through, and not presume that we know. They need to be allowed to tell us their story and experience that we are with them in their unfolding of that story. As they tell the story a *transformation* can take place. We may not notice it because it is taking place deep within the person.

They are getting a binding burden "off their chest"; our being willing to listen in a nonjudgmental and caring way creates the space for this release to take place. For our part this exchange must be explicitly grounded in *faith*. We need to be aware that Christ is meeting Christ, that Christ is ministering through us and that we, in turn, are being ministered to. And we allow our awareness to influence what we do and say, how we act.

This is quite a powerful insight. I know at times we find ourselves in a situation when the emotions can get very worked up. Sometimes we are filled with tensions and reactions. I find it helpful to keep in mind Shea's three key words: actual, transformation, and faith. The *actual* to remind myself to listen to all the details even if I can predict what is going to be said, to realize there is something I can always learn. *Transformation* reminds me that by my listening in a caring, nonjudgmental way, there is a chance that a healing will take place, that there can be some resolution in the case. Or if there isn't, there will be created a chance to continue the encounter at another time. *Faith* reminds me that I am in the middle of mystery, that this is a Spirit-filled event and that I want to be open to it and not get in the way of the Spirit.

Undoubtedly, one of the most impressive and powerful ministers in our world today is that little Yugoslavian-born sister, Mother Teresa. My coauthor, Father Basil, had an opportunity to visit with her recently. As he was leaving he asked her for a word to take back to his brothers at the abbey. Mother looked at him intently with her deep welcoming brown eyes and said with much emphasis: "Tell them to pray that *I do not get in God's way.*"

Perhaps at this point you might like to take a few moments to recall a recent experience you had in your ministry and look at it in the light of these three concepts: actual, transformation, and faith. Were they present in your ministry? What would you, perhaps, do differently the next time?

The process I have been sharing, it seems to me, can

be applied to any ministerial service. However, all of our service must always be grounded in the broader view, one that looks to our total growth in Christ. *We need a wholeness, whole-seeing* (more on this shortly), *and the power to be in the present moment.*

Jesus said, "I came that they might have life and have it to the full" (John 10:10). Nothing pleases the Lord more than a priest fully alive, just as nothing pleased God the Father more than Jesus fully alive. Jesus was very conscious of what pleased the Father. Often, in the course of his ministry, he went off to be alone with the Father. On occasion, he asked some of his friends to go apart with him. He knew he needed to have time and space apart in order to commune with his Father. He also needed time and space with his friends in order to build with them a support community. We, too, need to go apart, at times alone with the Father, at times with our friends.

By taking time to be alone with God, we not only cultivate that primary relationship, fundamental to any human life and the meaning of our celibacy, we also become aware of the fact that in all the events of our lives, God speaks to us and makes us more alive through them, whether they be social, physical, intellectual, emotional, or spiritual. He touches our being, and at all levels. For this reason we want to be sensitive to all our genuine needs. We need a social life. We have to make time for it. We need to watch over our physical well-being. We cannot function without a body, and we can be greatly impeded with a malfunctioning body. We need intellectual activity; we need to respond to the hunger of a mind made to know all things. Nor can we ignore our emotional needs, or we will pay the consequences. Fidelity to the spiritual journey must embrace, integrate, and respond to all of our legitimate needs.

We bring our desire to be close to Christ and our desire to be whole to our relationships with others, and especially to our support groups, where we look for and can find the help we need to keep faithfully on the journey toward *wholeness*. If we listen, we will find that our people want to support us in all of this. They sometimes seem to have a better sense than we do as to how much we need to take time and space for ourselves, to attend to our needs, to be with our friends, and to gather with our fellow priests so that we can be refueled and enlivened. There was a time when the "dedicated" priest never took time off to attend to his own needs: he was always there for his people. Today it's the "dedicated" priest who realizes that he does need time for himself, for he cannot give what he does not have. Holiness demands wholeness, for only then can the priest offer himself totally to the Lord and through the Lord to the people.

Whole persons need *whole-seeing*, the ability to see events, individuals, and institutions as part of the larger picture. Whole-seeing gives us a fresh outlook on things. It engenders an awareness that allows us to relax and be open to the inspirations of the moment. Most of us have spent too much time approaching life in an analytical way. It is the way in which we were trained. We believed that when we had reasoned something through we knew all that needed to be known about it. We have not allowed ourselves to be creative, to allow intuition to play its part in our seeing.

Whole-seeing calls us to live with paradox. All things are not black and white — God is found also in gray areas. Let me use an example that I have found helpful. Looking at life there is in us a Republican, a Democrat, and a mystic. The Republican in us believes that everyone can do on his own the things that he needs to do if only he is strong. We will help make him stronger. We will build him up and then let him be. The Democrat in us believes that everything will be okay if we can get people and events into a proper setting. Create the proper environment and all will go well. In reality, we know we cannot do everything on our own, no matter what be our strength. Moreover, our experiences have taught us that we are not as strong as we perhaps once thought we were. We do need the love, support, and help of others.

We also know from experience that ideal surroundings do not necessarily create success. We remember that change of assignment to that ideal place — it didn't turn out quite like we expected. We could hardly wait to move again.

But then there is in us the mystic. This mystical dimension makes us know that there is more to life than what is perceived by the Republican and the Democrat. All the events of our life fit into a broader picture; within them a greater power is at work. The development of our ability to see events as part of a larger picture and to see the greater power that is at work within them requires of us a special discipline, the discipline of meditation and contemplation. Through a contemplative prayer, such as Centering Prayer, we come to whole-seeing. In such a prayer we learn to slow down, rest awhile, allow the grace of God to flow in and through us as we surrender to God. We say to him: "Here I am, Lord. Without you I can do nothing. You hold the power to make fruitful what I am about. Let me never lose sight of the total picture as I do what I can." The Holy Spirit, acting through the gifts given us at baptism, enables us to see the whole picture: all things in God and God in all things. We begin to think, act, and live in that Love.

This is actually *being in the present moment*. The practice of the present moment may seem at first to be limiting. In fact, it is very freeing. To focus on the present moment frees us from being in the past and frees us from being in the future. When we are caught up in those imaginary worlds, we lose ourselves. And when we lose ourselves, we lose touch with reality. We can certainly learn from the past — it would be foolish not to. We can plan for the future — it would be foolish not to. But to live in the past is to live in illusion. Nor do we want to live in the future. It is no more real. It, too, is an illusion. Concerns and fears about the future sap our energies and deprive us from being fully alive now. This is the challenge: to guard our freedom by living in reality and in the fullness of the present moment.

This last point may seem to be quite theoretical. It was a word of wisdom I received back in the seminary from my spiritual director, a man in his seventies, that made this very practical for me. He said: "As I look back on my life I have come to the conclusion that God's plans for me were in the interruptions of my life, not in my plans and schedule." I have discovered through the years that too often I have missed God present in the interruptions because I have not been there, in the present reality. I was off in the future, the things I had scheduled to do, or in the past, when I planned everything out. If much of our life in ministry consists of interruptions, then how powerful it is to be able to be fully present to the interruptions without being distracted by what has been interrupted. What a loss it is to go through a day and never truly be present to what is really going on because our minds are cluttered with the past and the future.

Being aware of our need for wholeness, we see how time alone with God and time with significant persons is very important. We seek in this time, through contemplative prayer, that whole-seeing which keeps us from isolating events so that we see them always as part of a larger picture, see them as they really are, in Christ and in the mysterious work of forming a people whom we call Church. With this more integrated perspective we find all in the present moment; the past and the future no longer hold us back from being fully available to what is present. With such dispositions, we are ready to minister like our Master, eager to serve and not to be served.

I would like to end these reflections on the spirituality of ministry with words from two of our American cardinals. "A Reflection on Life-Long Learning," written by Cardinal John F. Dearden, tells us:

> It helps now and then to step back and take the long view. The kingdom is not only beyond our efforts, it is beyond our vision. We accomplish in our lifetime only a tiny fraction of the magnificent enterprise that is the Lord's work. . . . Nothing we do is complete, which is another way of saying that the

kingdom always lies beyond us. No sermon says all that should be said. No prayer fully expresses our faith. No confession brings perfection. No pastoral visit brings wholeness. No program accomplishes the Church's mission. No set of goals and objectives includes everything. This is what we are about. We plant seed that one day will grow. We water seeds already planted knowing that they hold future promises. We lay foundations that will need further development. We provide yeast that produces effects far beyond our capabilities. . . . We cannot do everything, and there is a sense of liberation in realizing that. This enables us to do something and do it very, very well. It may be incomplete, but it is a beginning, a step along the way, an opportunity for the Lord's grace to enter and do the rest. We may never see the end results, but that is the difference between the master builder and the worker. We are the workers, not the master builders . . . ministers not messiahs. . . . We are prophets of a future that is not our own.

And finally, this witness from Cardinal Joseph L. Bernardin:

About seven years ago [this was written in 1983], I came to understand that the pace of my life and the direction of my activity were unfocused, uncentered in a significant way. This created a certain unrest. I came to realize that I needed to make some changes in my life, and chief among these was a renewal of personal prayer.

Mention of prayer may evoke an image of "saying" prayers, of reciting formulas. I mean something quite different. When we speak of the renewal of prayer in our lives, we are speaking of reconnecting ourselves with the larger mystery of life and of our common existence. This implies becoming disciplined in the use of our time, in the use of Centering Prayer, and in the development of a contemplative stance toward life.

When this happens, we begin to experience healing, integration, wholeness, peacefulness. We begin to hear more clearly the echoes of the Word in our own lives, in our own hearts. And as that Word takes root in the depths of our being, it begins to grow and to transform the way we live. It affects our relationships with people around us and above all our relationship with the Lord. From this rootedness flow our energies, our ministry, our ways of loving. From this core we can proclaim the Lord Jesus and his Gospel not only with faith and conviction but also with love and compassion.

7

A Father

●

Everybody Calls Me Father was a popular book making the rounds when I was in the seminary. I am afraid I don't remember the author or anything else about the book except its catchy title. There was a time when that was quite so in regard to priests — at least to their face. It is certainly less so today. Many a good lay person, hoping to narrow the painful gap between clergy and laity, prefers to be much less formal. And many priests encourage this. Others, in these ecumenical days, are influenced by Protestant mores or a stronger fundamental interpretation of the Scripture: "Call no man your father on earth" (Matthew 23:9). And then, too, many of us appear less frequently in the "uniform" that called forth the "Good morning, Father."

Yet many do still call us Father. The expectations of even more are that we do fulfill a fatherly role in their regard. It has sometimes been said we are a generation without fathers. Anyone in ministry is deeply and painfully aware of the vast number who have grown up and are growing up without the physical or emotional presence of a father. There are many, many consciously or unconsciously in search of a father.

In fact, every person is in search of a father, and rightly so. We have been baptized into Christ: "It is no longer I who live, but Christ who lives in me" (Galatians 2:20). I am a son, and, like Christ, my whole being is essentially "to the Father." Christian life can be summed up as an appropriation of the Christ-nature given in baptism and the living-out of that in seeking the Father.

Our natural parents should be for us the first sacrament of the Father and of his love in our lives. All too often this is not the case, or it is not carried through in the fullness it should be. So most of us need another father. We, as spiritual fathers, have a lot of fathering to do, today perhaps more than ever. Too few of our parishioners (I will use the term parishioners here — because the largest number of priests are in parochial ministry — but the word stands equally for students, patients, religious sisters, or whatever other group or groups to whom we are called to minister) have had a very good experience of paternity exercised on their behalf. We priests will find ourselves being called to make up something of what was wanting in natural parents, even as we seek also to go beyond that into the ministry of spiritual paternity. We will have to be able to bring to our ministry a lot of human warmth and love and affirmation. On top of that, we will have to call our "sons" and "daughters" into the fullness of adoptive divine filiation. We will want always to remember that ours is a sacramental role. When we have done what is needed from us, we will step aside and let our sons and daughters be wholly to *the* Father.

At the same time, as we minister we will be ministered unto. Whether we are called Father or not, we still have a need to experience generativity in our lives. This is a deep human need. Erik Erikson's *Stages of Life* has made us more reflectively and perhaps more acutely aware of this. For him this is the keynote of adult life, that long period which stretches from thirty-five to sixty-five. We have a need to be a part of establishing and guiding the next generation in ways that create life and pass it on. Having forgone the usual human experience of this, with Christ and in deepest union with him, we are called to be fathers of the world to come — to exercise a spiritual paternity. Part of the emptiness and pain in the lives of many of us is a lack of this sense of being generative, made mockery of when people repeatedly call us "Father" and we seem to be fathering no one. Actually though, as priests the opportunity to exercise this service is ours in a specially ample and fulfilling way.

A great spiritual father on Mount Athos, the center of Orthodox monasticism and indeed the spiritual center of the whole Orthodox Church, once remarked to me: "Spiritual paternity is different from natural paternity. In natural paternity it is the father who decides to beget a son. In spiritual paternity it is the son who comes and calls forth the father." Men and women will come and call us forth to serve them as spiritual fathers only if they perceive an openness on our part to serve them in this way, and only if they perceive a fullness of life in us that gives them hope that we can help generate fuller life in them. As pastors many will be coming to us precisely looking to us to help call forth the Christ-life in them. As spiritual fathers our gift of ourselves in love to our parishioners should be no less total than that of a good natural father; indeed, it should be even fuller.

I suspect some of us might be inclined to react a bit against the concept of ourselves as spiritual fathers. The term could negate the kind of adult relationship that we are seeking to foster with our people. There has been a general reaction against the paternalism that dominated so much of the Church and religious life, and, unfortunately, is still found in some corners. We certainly do not want to foster any paternalistic attitudes. Another factor is that many of our parishioners have had such a bad experience of their own fathers or they have been so portrayed to them by very hurt mothers, that the concept is totally distorted. Nonetheless, such parishioners seek the reality which they have never known but which is a naturally sought ingredient of life. We must take care to really listen to our people, and certainly not project on them any of our own personal reactions or hang-ups. We want to respond to their real needs and legitimate desires. We do not want to promote paternalism; we want truly adult relations where we are responding to adults. We do want to exercise and live a true spiritual, sacramental, and life-giving paternity, making present God the Father's love and care.

One of the main obstacles to our doing this may well be an anger or resentment we ourselves still harbor in our hearts toward our own father. This should not surprise us. We do not need to repress such feelings. Our fathers (and mothers), like ourselves, are poor weak sinners, wounded persons, at the effect of their parents and environment. They have, in fact, failed us in many ways, some very obvious perhaps (such as child abuse, desertion, and alcoholism), others more subtle (like emotional deprivation). We need to face these facts — alone or in converse with another — accept them and let them go, forgiving our parents from our hearts and expressing this as well as we can. Then with a new freedom we can let the Lord heal all the wounds of these bad memories and we can begin to give our parents all the love they deserve. In this freedom we will also find the freedom we need to be truly paternal toward others.

Let us now look a little bit more at what precisely are the elements in this ministry of spiritual paternity. My understanding is drawn from our Christian tradition, a part of the tradition still very much alive among the Christian communities of the East where I have come more fully into contact with it. This is true even among our Eastern-rite brothers and sisters here in the United States. I can remember being especially touched by the warm, loving, fatherly way in which Bishop Joseph Zyach, the Maronite bishop from Brooklyn, greeted his priests in the course of a national gathering of bishops.

Above all, the spiritual father is *a sacrament of*

God the Father, a sacrament of his paternity and maternity. In a sense, it might be better to speak of "spiritual parenthood," but that abstract word lacks the very quality of warmth and incarnation that is of the essence in this role. The Scriptures make it patently evident that God's care for us is tenderly maternal as well as strongly paternal. It also has the intimacy of a lover; we will speak of that later.

As spiritual fathers supplementing — sometimes totally replacing — the natural father's and mother's spiritual ministry, we are to make God the Father present to the persons who turn to us. Our response is to be that of the Father: his love, his concern, his calling forth, his affirmation, his confirmation, the demands that his being and love make. To so respond, we obviously have to know the Father and know him intimately. But "no one knows the Father except the Son and any one to whom the Son chooses to reveal him" (Matthew 11:27). To fulfill our role we want to be men who have intimate communication with the Son so that the Son can reveal the Father to us, can help us to understand the Father and the Father's response to his children. This is one of the reasons why a very important element in our lives is a daily meeting with Christ in the Gospels, listening to him, letting him speak to us about the Father. We want to listen, again and again, to those texts where Jesus speaks of the Father and his relation with him. Gradually the full import of these revealing words will sink in and form our minds and hearts so that we begin to respond to those who turn to us in the way the Father would respond to them. It will often happen that it will be in today's prayer that we learn how to respond as the Father to the parishioner who comes to us today. Our Lord, using a negative expression to convey a positive reality, said: "Let the day's own trouble be sufficient for the day" (Matthew 6:34). He gives us each day the grace, the insight, we need for the day. We cannot afford to miss our daily encounter with the Lord, if we want to be prepared for the demands of the day.

We want to remember that the spiritual father's ministry is a sacramental one. He is a sacrament of the Father's presence and love. Sacraments must give way to reality. As spiritual fathers we want to be sensitive and perceive when it is time for us to give way. At times the ministry of a spiritual father is a transient one in regard to a particular parishioner. Our ministry terminates as the parishioner turns to another. Sometimes, too, we are the ones to perceive it is time for a change; it is time to direct our friend to another. We want to be ready to let go and let the other begin to fulfill this sacramental role without causing the confusing situation where two are trying to minister to the same person in the same way, superimposing one sign upon another so that neither is clear. This ministry of spiritual paternity calls for a particular detachment. We can be called upon to give a great deal of ourselves to a particular person and then be expected to simply let that person walk away. We must be careful that there is no subtle hanging on and no hidden or overt jealousy. This all calls for a certain largeness of spirit, something truly generative.

It is true that tradition calls for a certain permanence in this relationship. In the East a young person will go in search of a spiritual father, and finding him, will remain with him until death separates them — at least physically, for the spiritual bond grows more intimate after death intervenes. (Perhaps I should not even say physically, for the spiritual son will often preserve with reverent care some relic of his father. I have been invited to venerate the skull of more than one spiritual father.) Yet even when the relationship perdures, the father wants to take care not to stand in the way of his disciple's entering into immediate relation with God the Father. He does not want to be more present as a sacrament than is truly needed.

The spiritual father is also *a sacrament of Jesus Christ*. Christ is father ("the Father of the world to come" is the way the *Douay Version* puts it in Isaiah 9:6). The spiritual father is to be a Christ-person, one whom the Christian disciple can follow, knowing that in so doing he is following Christ. Saint Paul affirms with no uncertainty his own spiritual paternity: "Granted you have ten thousand guardians in Christ, you have only one father. It was I who begot you in Christ Jesus through my preaching of the gospel" (1 Corinthians 4:15); and he dares to go on to say: "Be imitators of me, as I am of Christ" (1 Corinthians 11:1). I don't know how many of us would dare to say that. What we want to be able to say is more like this: Be imitators of me as one who is trying to be a wholehearted follower of Jesus Christ. It is in the trying that we give the example. And it is the example that our parishioners need. The finished product, the perfect disciple, might be too far ahead to be followed; it could be discouraging to try to follow such a one — though I hesitate to make a generalization of that, since I see many flocking to follow Mother Teresa as a spiritual mother. We could hardly find a more perfect disciple of Jesus than this tough, loving little woman.

As spiritual fathers we need to have the mind of Christ: "Have this mind among yourselves, which was in Christ Jesus" (Philippians 2:5). This is not just a question of the intellect or the understanding, but of a whole life-attitude: the heart of Christ, the inner feel of Christ; in this particular instance, the feeling of Christ for each person who presents him- or herself to us. We do want to see Christ in our people and respond to them as we would to Christ. But we also want to be Christ to them and respond to them as Christ responds to them: with love and compassion, taking on their pains, their aches, their needs, their sins.

Here let me say again, to fulfill our role as fathers, we need to encounter Christ daily in a most intimate, listening, learning way. We want to let the Gospels speak to our hearts and form them, form this mind of Christ in us, so that we spontaneously, as it were, respond to those who come to us in the way he would respond. To be good Christian spiritual fathers we will spend a lot of time with the Gospels, with Christ in the Gospels. This is essential. If our ministry is not as fruitful as we would like it to be, this is the first thing we should check: Are we regularly spending *a truly significant amount of time* with Christ, letting him form our minds and hearts?

The spiritual father's own practice of deep prayer and his ability to teach his people how to pray enters very much into his service of them.

We need a deep, strengthening, ever-renewing relation with our blessed Lord if we are not only to sustain and respond to all the demands of our service but also if we are going to be able to do it with enthusiasm and joy. Our own lives, as men who have chosen celibacy for the love of the Savior, will not be fulfilled if we do not enjoy an ever growing love-relation with our Chosen One. If we ourselves do not find deep satisfaction, joy, and fulfillment in our lives — and a deep love-relation is essential for this — we can hardly hope to convey to others that this way of Christian discipleship is a life really worth considering.

If we are regularly meeting our Lord in the depths of our being where we are coming forth from the Father's creative love, this will have important consequences for our ministry as fathers. Constantly experiencing ourselves as being so totally affirmed (the very God of heaven and earth at every moment is present, affirming us by the very gift of life and shared divine life), all defensiveness melts away from us. We can be a totally open person to those to whom we minister. Parishioners will very quickly sense this and will feel free, in their turn, to be totally open with us. Moreover, being in touch with the Creative Love from which we come forth, we will experience the reality that not only we but all those to whom we are ministering are constantly coming forth from that love. We will deeply sense our oneness with all and thus feel a deep compassion and oneness with them. It will be easy to love them. We will instinctively respond with a very caring love to each one who comes. And when parishioners experience such a reception, they will really know that this father is with them in their quest for meaning and life. They will have confidence, and an open relation can fruitfully blossom.

Moreover, if we actually teach our parishioners Christian meditation or how to be open to the experience of God through Centering Prayer, we will help them to get in touch with their deepest self and with the grace they are receiving. Essentially, Christian life lies in the appropriation of the grace we are receiving, the grace to be Christ, the Son, to the Father in that bond of love who is the Holy Spirit of them both. Deep prayer helps the parishioners to perceive the grace they are receiving. But they need to see it alive in another if they are to be able to identify it. We need to be in touch with the grace we are receiving and be living out of it so that the parishioners can understand to what they are being called. Deep prayer, then, is important for both us spiritual fathers and for our people. When we meditate together, wonderful things happen.

I should perhaps inject an incidental note here. Today, in our ministry, we have something of a semantic problem. In our recent Christian tradition the word "meditation" usually signifies a discursive type of consideration evoking affections and resolutions, while "contemplation" refers to that kind of prayer where one leaves thinking behind and simply responds to the Reality. Among our Hindu brothers and sisters these terms are used in exactly the opposite way. "Contemplation" is for them the discursive work, "meditation" is the wordless presence. It is perhaps a sad commentary on our failure to live and share our own tradition, but today, even in America, it is largely the Hindu terminology that prevails. We need to be aware of this when people speak to us about meditation. They probably mean a contemplative practice.

The spiritual father is also *a mediator*, standing before the Father with his people in his heart, presenting them and all their needs to the Father. When we pray, God does not listen to our lips, he looks to our hearts. We want to take those who come to us into our hearts, into our care and concern. We cannot fool them in this regard and we certainly cannot fool God. We stand before the Father with them in our hearts, obtaining for them from the Father that gift of life which they seek.

This does mean spending time in explicit prayer for our people. And more important, it means that our people are in fact people whom we know and love and care about. They cannot be just so many names on the register. In this ministry our relationship with our people is important.

A few practical thoughts that flow from this: Our initial response to a person, to an inquirer, is important. First impressions are lasting impressions. It would be sad if this response was institutional or impersonal, rather than a warm, Christlike, personal one to the full extent that the situation allows. To respond to an inquiry with a printed letter or even with a personal word that gets kind of lost in a large packet of printed stuff is getting off on the wrong foot. What we are concerned about is developing a loving relation in the Lord, a community in Christ, a true friendship that we hope will perdure forever. Friendships do not usually begin with a lot of forms. I think if we are honest we will admit that the forms do not really tell us that much. The factual data we need can be picked up later. If a person turns to us, is it not an indication that the Lord has some role for us to play in this person's life, even if it be a transient one? To be for a moment a sacrament of God's love to another is a great privilege and can have eternal impact. To let someone into our hearts is to begin something that will blossom in eternity, whatever its course in this life.

Public words, pastoral messages, or letters, even in the case of the best and most open of us, offer a very limited basis for the kind of friendship in the Lord that we want to develop with our people as a spiritual father. Visits to the homes have value. But an intimate sharing cannot readily take place in shared quarters. We need to have a space, an inviting place that is perceived as wide open and welcoming to any who want to come, a place they can identify with as their place in the community where they can find their spiritual father. This may well be in the rectory itself or monastery, though the priest needs to keep his private place. In such a space the spiritual father and the parishioner can comfortably get to know each other and explore the heart in its depths to discern what the Lord is saying. Time and space are needed for a relationship to grow. The behavioral sciences have made us aware of the importance of a supportive and proportionate environment.

As a spiritual father gets to know and love his people, because he is a man of faith in communion with the Father, mediation of the most effective sort cannot but follow.

Another dimension of our ministry of spiritual paternity is that of *example*. A father begets a son in his own image, and through education, in its strictest and most natural sense, forms him to his own likeness. If the spiritual father is fulfilling the aspects of his role of which we have already spoken, he will be fulfilling what is most essential here. He will be giving example of what is at the heart of every Christian life, and, *a fortiori*, every priestly life: an intimate relation with God in Christ, which involves that dedicated, loving listening that forms the person and his response.

Even though all are called to intimacy with God, the priest is called in a special way. All are called to be lovers. God is love. We are to be like him, made in his image. For most men the primary school of love is an intimate relation with a woman. This love, with its mutuality, is to be for the man and woman first of all, but also for others, a sacrament and an expression of their love for God. For the one called to celibacy for the kingdom, the intimate love of his life is God in Jesus Christ. If such intimacy is not fostered by the celibate, he will be a truncated human being, or he will seek undue intimacy elsewhere, to the peril of his celibacy and all that it really means. As spiritual fathers, in all that we say, do, and are, we want to give witness that this is the orientation of our lives. If we are to be generative of life, it will be because of a fruitfulness in Christ Jesus. Our parental love will be one with that of the Father and Jesus, because of our bond of love with them. Thus we will seek to exemplify for our people the kind of love life that is to be sought. Moreover, we want to be exemplars who can teach. From our own life experience we want to be able to share with the parishioner how one cultivates this love-relation with the Lord. In practice we will need to develop or find simple methods that the parishioner can begin to use to encounter the Lord in the Scriptures — methods simple enough and flexible enough to open out, in due time, into a full, intimate, contemplative sharing with the Lord. There are many simple methods of Gospel prayer offered today. Centering Prayer, for one, is a simple way to move into quiet contemplative prayer.

Besides being an example of this basic Christian relationship, as priests we want to exemplify a particular image of the Christ-life, that which we identify as the charism of our particular call. This is extremely important for our ministry. If a young man is receiving the grace of this particular vocation, he can identify it only if he sees it living in someone. This means, then, that we as spiritual fathers need to be very much who we are — priests of Jesus Christ; and if we are religious, members of our institute sharing in the charism of our particular founder. This will be so only if we have deeply imbibed the spirit of our vocation and have lived it with fidelity. This dimension of our spiritual paternity, engendering others to share in our particular call and to be there to carry it on after us, is a special blessing for us in that it challenges us in a special way to live out of the fullness of who we are in Christ, the whole Christ with his particular members, each with its own function and revelation of the beauty of the Head.

In speaking about our role as mediator I have already mentioned friendship with our people, but let me speak more explicitly about this particular aspect of the spiritual father's role — that of being *friend*. If the parishioners are in some respects our spiritual sons and daughters, they are adult sons and daughters. An adult son or daughter is a friend. This is one of the important aspects of becoming an adult. A child must in some way break away from his or her parents, only to return to them to form with them a new relation, an adult relation, where he or she begins to take responsibility for them, a responsibility that grows with the years and which cannot be set aside by a priestly or religious vocation — our Lord has made that very clear (see Mark 7:9-13).

As the parishioners' relationship with us as spiritual father grows, the sharing will become more mutual. The parishioners will grow in their own loving concern for us and will pray more for us. And they will also share more in our concerns. They will be able to enter deeply into our ministry, not only through prayer for the other parishioners, but also through friendship with them, through encouragement, and mutual sharing. The parishioners can share our labor, whether it be the practical housekeeping and office tasks or more spiritual ones.

Finally, the spiritual father is to be a *reflective guide*. It is certainly true that the role of guidance is not restricted to a spiritual father. It is also true that any Christian who is responding to his brother or sister as a guide (or director, to use a term commonly used, but which I do not like because of the assumed authority that has too often crept into such a relationship) will also bring into his relation in various degrees the qualities we have already discussed. But the spiritual paternity has a fullness of caring and responsibility that goes beyond that of fraternal Christian guidance. Some priests would prefer to avoid paternal concepts and attitudes and stay at the level of guidance. But we should always keep in mind that our ministry is one of service. If our people are seeking something more from us, we want to respond and not let our own hesitations or hang-ups hold us back.

I speak of *reflective* guidance. This needs to be understood in two senses. We want to be reflective in the sense of pondering deeply in prayer, in the light of the

Gospels, on all that we perceive in our contact with the parishioner. Very serious and prolonged reflection in this sense is incumbent upon us. But we want also to be reflective in the sense of reflecting back to the parishioner as purely and clearly as possible what we hear and see the Holy Spirit saying and doing in them. We want to be a bright and undistorted mirror for the parishioner. This calls for detachment and purity of heart on our part. Our own natural feelings and reactions have to be discerned so that the image we send back to the parishioner is not distorted.

Both of these processes of reflection call for a careful, open, and attentive listening. We want to provide a climate of compassionate attentiveness that will invite the parishioner to bring to the surface all the stirrings that are in his or her heart: the wonder, the fears, the longings, the passions, so that he himself can see them clearly in this mirror and evaluate them in an unpressured space and with compassionate assistance.

We are guides, not directors. We are to guide parishioners in listening and responding to the Holy Spirit, who alone has the authority to direct the human person, the child of God.

The question of obedience might be considered here. The stories from the Fathers of the Desert and the practice of some Fathers among the Eastern monastics even today might raise the question of blind obedience to the spiritual father. The father is a sacrament of God the Father. *When it is clear what God wants* in a particular instance, the only adequate response is complete, unquestioning obedience. Unfortunately, in most cases it is not so clear what God wants of us. Also, we must always remember that vocation is an invitation, a conditional invitation: "*If* you would be perfect. . . ." It seems to be also (though not everyone will agree with me in this) that at times and perhaps oftentimes, God in his lavish generosity invites one to several possible paths, leaving to the freedom of his beloved one the option of which one he should choose. The greatest gift God has given to us is our freedom, the power to love. And God profoundly respects this freedom. Certainly, the spiritual father wants to fully reverence and respect the freedom of each parishioner.

As important as the paternal dimension is in our ministry I think a few words of caution are not out of place. It is something I have already touched upon — the importance of detachment. As spiritual fathers we want always to be on the watch that in our relationship with our sons and daughters we are not in any way using them to fulfill our own needs. Every man does need to be generative. In actuality, the ministry of spiritual paternity will fulfill this need in us. But nothing could frustrate the fruitfulness of our ministry as much, or do so much harm, as seeking primarily our own fulfillment and using others for this end. Our ministry, our relation with the parishioners, must be wholly oriented toward the parishioners' well-being and growth. In doing this we ourselves will grow.

As we have reflected on all that is involved in the ministry of a spiritual father I am sure you have had the reaction: "This is impossible to fulfill with the hundreds of people who have been entrusted to my care." It is. But then not every parishioner will call us forth as a spiritual father in any full sense. Remember what the spiritual father from Mount Athos said: "In this matter of spiritual paternity it is the son who calls forth the father." When I first became a superior, a wise old superior wrote to me: "Remember, you cannot reach everyone." True! Not everyone will relate happily with us. We want to realize this and accept it peacefully. But if we are truly open, loving, and welcoming men, we will almost certainly be inundated with those who are seeking. What are we to do?

Some years ago a friend of mine was elected overseer of one of the Protestant churches. After an initial acquaintance with his diocese, or constituency, he placed a subordinate in charge of the day-to-day matters and set out to spend some time in each parish. He was seeking a breakthrough in regard to effective ministry.

He brought to his quest a doctorate in theology and in sociology. When the eight-month quest was over, he shared with me the insight he had attained: it was one basically of our failure to see the obvious. The answer was so obvious, or should be for any follower of Christ. We should do as he did. While attending to the needs of the masses, Jesus selected twelve of those who came to him seeking to be his disciples, and to these twelve he gave special time and attention. In time they would be able to carry forth his ministry. So, too, the pastor can choose from among those who are calling him forth as a spiritual father a limited number, perhaps especially among the young adults who are often the most neglected in our parishes and so often lost to the Church. While responding to the rest as best he can with his limits of time and energy, he can give to this select group his full care as a spiritual father. Soon enough they will be able to lend a hand in ministry to the large community. And, please God, some of them will identify in their own hearts the grace to follow their spiritual father more fully in responding to a call to the priestly life and ministry, becoming themselves spiritual fathers. Can we pattern our ministry on a better exemplar than the Lord Jesus himself?

Before concluding let me add another oblique note here. It is of primary importance that we as spiritual fathers know and live our own tradition, and know how to teach it to those who come to us. A simple method of scriptural prayer, the rosary and stations, Centering Prayer, and the prayer of the hours are all ours to be shared with our people. We should be able to discern when and how to teach them. We need to put out our shingles as teachers of Christian meditation so that our young do not need to go to other traditions to learn what they so richly have in our own. But we need, too, to be familiar with other traditions and practices. Many of those coming to us have had such experience. It is often an experience of this kind that first awakens a dormant spiritual life and brings them back to seek a fuller practice of their Christian faith, and even opens them to religious or priestly life. We need to be able to respond to the values they have found, give sympathetic understanding to these, and help them integrate what is of permanent value into the fullness of Christian experience. I do not think this can be done from a mere "book knowledge." Besides, some experience of other practices can help us to understand, appreciate, and practice our own traditions the better. Taking the time and effort to have such experiences will invigorate our lives, making us more open, more truly catholic. If it is possible, it would be good for us to go to a Zen center and do some sitting or take part in a *seshein* (a Zen retreat). Reading Father William Johnson would be a good preparation for this but would never teach us as much as some actual sitting. For yoga — if we cannot find some courses locally, or if we cringe at the thought of displaying ourselves in such postures (who knows? your presence might be the way some will find their way back to Christ and his Church) — we can use Father Dechanet's little paperback *Yoga in Ten Lessons* and begin in the privacy of our own rooms. We might find the *asanas* very invigorating and the *pranyama* might help us to get control of our smoking — if we have need there. (Many today are turned off by a priest whose office is filled with stale and even unhealthy air. If you are a smoker, you might never hear this; but if you are a nonsmoker, you hear it about others readily enough.) It might be difficult today to be initiated into TM (transcendental meditation), but we can get some idea of the TM experience by working with Benson's *Relaxation Response*. (Read also his *After the Relaxation Response* — a fascinating witness from an agnostic.) Ira Progoff's *Intensive Journal* is also popular today and helping many with its various processes, including some aimed at deep meditation. Even more American — that is, eclectic — is *The Forum*, successor to Werner Erhard's *est*, a two-weekend program that has opened new space in many people's lives and has given them the freedom for a deeper life of faith. Since weekends are difficult for most in ministry, a special program has been devised that places some of the more effective techniques of *The Forum* in the hands of those whose lives are about sacred ministry and allows these experiences to blossom into contemplative experience through Centering Prayer. The Mastery Foundation offers five-day courses for those who minister: *To Make a Difference.*

Opening ourselves to a variety of experiences can make us more open men. Going through them can put us in closer touch with some of the experiences that have shaped the minds and hearts of those who are coming to us. Letting our own spiritual life be confronted by these vital currents can lead to a vitalization of our own prayer life. We obviously cannot begin to practice in an ongoing fashion such an assortment of exercises, but even a relatively brief experience of them will enable us to come at them "from inside" when a parishioner begins to share his or her experience with us. It seems to me that this giving of our time and energy to such programs is part of that "laying down" of our lives for others, for the people we are specifically called to serve as spiritual fathers.

I have touched on only a few aspects of our ministry as spiritual fathers, though I believe they are very important and central aspects. There are, of course, other elements that are very important also. For instance, that life we mediate is the life entrusted to, and lived out in, community, and so our relation and that of our people with the community is of the greatest importance. Ours is also an ecclesial life, a special participation in and building up of the life of the whole Body of Christ, and so our relationship with the Church universal in its fullness is again of very great importance. We must have identified our own role in the Church and community and be able to help our people to perceive the ecclesial meaning of the role they are being invited to live. Then there are other aspects we might consider: our relation with Mary, the mystery (and it is a mystery) of truly Christian poverty, and so on.

It is a tremendous grace to be called to serve another

as spiritual father, to be to him or her a sacrament of the Father and of the Lord Jesus, and to be invited to share a deep, intimate, spiritual friendship. It is also a humbling grace, a very humbling one, and a painful one. For we cannot but experience how much we fail to be indeed an unsullied transparent sacrament, a fitting exemplar, an effective and faithful mediator. There is deep pain in the realization that our people suffer because of our limitations and infidelities. We beg the Lord insistently to make up for this. We know that, in part, the lack of an abundance of priestly vocations rests upon us. Despondency, of course, is not the proper response to these realizations. Rather, the proper response is to bear the pain redemptively with Christ so that it will lead to our own healing and the healing of others, and to fruitfulness in the future. If we are humble enough to accept the fact that fruitfulness is not our due, but the pure gift of the superabundance of an all-loving God, then he can give us a fruitfulness beyond all our expectations. A vocation to be a father in the spirit, evoking a recognition, calling forth, nurturing a gift of life, a participation in the life we have received in our own calling — that is how I see the ministry of the spiritual father. Anything that can help us to be more fully in touch with the life we have received and to live it more fully; anything that can help us touch more intimately, more empathetically, the currents of life in those we serve — this is what we want to exploit to the full.

8

Friendship

One of the common tales told about voodoo deaths among tribes in Australia, Central Africa, and the Caribbean is this: When the tribe decides to punish one of its members because of a major betrayal, the witch doctor is called in. He takes a "magic bone" and points it at the guilty person and intones a chant that is supposed to cast a spell upon the miscreant. The other tribe members then know that they may have no further dealings with this unfortunate individual. The reported fact is that the person so cut off from the community withers and dies in a short period of time. Life disintegrates. With the withdrawal of the tribe's interaction and support, the individual cannot survive.

Karl Rahner argues that we come truly to know God only through relationships. Brother Charles of Jesus (Charles de Foucauld), the inspiration of the Jesu Caritas Fraternities, even though he himself spent much of his life in solitude, always insisted that one learns to love God by loving one's fellow humans. John, the beloved disciple, tells us: "In this the love of God was made manifest among us, that God sent his only Son into the world, so that we might live through him. In this is love, not that we loved God but that he loved us and sent his Son to be the expiation for our sins. Beloved, if God so loved us, we also ought to love one another. . . . We love, because he first loved us. If any one says, 'I love God,' and hates his brother, he is a liar; for he who does not love his brother whom he has seen, cannot love God whom he has not seen'' (1 John 4:9-11, 19-20).

In the Gospels we read that Jesus had many close relationships with women and men. His mission was to draw people close to the Father in drawing them to himself. Saint Paul, in his writings, goes out of his way to send his love not only to special groups of people but to many individuals — both women and men — whom he names and speaks of as close friends. He frequently uses phrases like ''who is dear to me in the Lord,'' and ''to my beloved.''

A sign of human maturity is the ability to enter into responsible relationships. Studies have unfortunately shown that we American priests are underdeveloped in this regard. Generally, we have not worked through the challenge of intimacy. As a result, our level of full human maturation is generally lower than that of men of comparable age in society as a whole. This does not necessarily detract from our personal holiness, but it does say something about our wholeness. We may well have a very high degree of dedication to the women and men whom we serve. But the studies indicate that even though this kind of dedicated love is present we often are unable to enter into and manifest that fuller human love which is the more actual expression of the divine.

One of the reasons why we hold back from allowing ourselves to be so totally with our people may well be that our faith is not as deep and perceptive as it should be. Perhaps we do not sufficiently understand or trust a Jesus who weeps at a friend's tomb before he raises him up, who lets a disciple rest his head upon his heart, and lets a woman hug and kiss his feet. Perhaps we let some of the ''detachment'' of this world's professionalism creep into our response to our people.

A priest-friend shared this deeply touching story with

144

me. It was years after it had taken place, but it continued to shape his life as a priest and it has certainly impacted on mine. Jim had just been assigned to his first parish, the oils still fresh on his hands. It was his very first night on duty. A call came from the local hospital regarding an auto accident involving some of the parish youths. When he arrived at the emergency ward, the medical staff and police officers were busy taking care of their respective duties. The four teenagers were dead. As Father looked on, feeling rather helpless, there was a commotion at the door. The police sergeant nudged Jim: "Those are the parents, Father. Will you take care of them?"

With the help of the patrolman, Jim herded the parents into a side room. The one father was shouting: "Why can't I see my kids? They are my kids!" He grabbed at Jim, yelling, "Why can't I see them?" Before he knew what he was saying, Jim blurted out: "Because they are dead." Everyone, including Jim, collapsed on the couches in a fit of sobs and tears.

As he tossed on his bed that night Jim felt like a first-class failure. All the others — the medical staff and police officers — had handled themselves so professionally. And he, instead of gently and lovingly breaking the horrible news to the parents — he had shocked them. And then he wasn't able to muster up any consoling thoughts. All his fine theology fled as he sat there crying with the grieved parents. How unprofessional! Was this the fruit of all his years of preparation for ministry? Was this the best he could do? He cried himself to sleep: crying for the parents, crying for their children, crying for himself.

The next day he received a call from the brother of one of the parents. The parents wanted him to come to do the wake service that evening. They weren't his parishioners, they belonged to a neighboring parish, but, of course, he would go. When he arrived at the funeral home, it was very crowded. The parents met him at the entrance and led him through the crowd toward the coffins. As he struggled to follow them he was aware of people pointing at him and whispering to their neighbors.

Everyone was aware of his gross failure. He felt worse and worse. Again he could not hold back the tears.

After the wake service the parents accompanied him to the door. The mother spoke: "Father, would it be possible . . . could you say the funeral Mass for our children?" Jim was dumbstruck. Why him? What about the pastor? Why this blubbering, incompetent kid of a priest? Then the uncle explained. The mother and father had told everyone about him. How much it meant to them that this man of God could sit with them in their hour of bitterest grief and instead of trying to offer some pious platitudes, wept with them, sharing fully their shock and pain. In him, Jesus was there as the truly compassionate, very human, consoling Savior. They wanted a priest like that to help them through the difficult hours ahead as they laid their two young ones to rest.

A superficial faith does not support us in allowing all the turmoil and pain of truly human emotions, of real caring, of all the elements of the human growing process to enter in so that a deeper relationship within God might be present among us and with our people.

I was tempted to remain on a more theoretical plane in writing this chapter about relationships and friendship. That seemed to me at first to be the better course. But I had an opportunity to sit down with some priest-friends to explore ideas. Unanimously they encouraged me to express myself freely and practically. With this encouragement from my friends, I want to share more deeply with you about relationships and friendship as a part of our spiritual journey. Celibacy is deeply involved in what I am about to share. However, we will reserve the explicit consideration of that sometimes problematic gift for the next chapter.

Let me make some preliminary observations before I go into the precise question of relationships in the Lord.

The priest is no longer "the Lone Ranger" — at least in most cases he does not want to be. The greater emphasis today is definitely on community. We find ourselves, more and more, working closely with others. As we do we find the question of special friendships surfacing. We might even find ourselves falling in love. Very quickly, in human relationships, we are challenged wth the reality of our sexuality. Some would say, challenged by sex; but in reality, what we are talking about is sexuality, human sexuality. Human sexuality is part of our God-given, natural power to relate to others in a caring and loving way. When we are comfortable with our sexuality and allow ourselves to be sexual persons, we can experience qualities such as feeling, warmth, openness, and mutual respect in our relationships with others. When we fear these qualities and avoid the kind of relationships in which they can arise, we lessen our ability to relate to others and truly love them. This, in turn, lessens our ability to relate to God and truly love him. To deny ourselves the opportunity to grow in these human, loving qualities can lead us to becoming frightened, threatened, or bitter men in our service of God. On the other hand, if we are truly alive with God's love, that love of which John the Beloved spoke, then we can be present to our people in that open, caring way that is so necessary for true ministry. Just reflect on the special moments you have shared with your people on their journeys: the preparations for marriage, the communion calls to the sick, the youth work, those special people you sat with as they died — so many special shared moments. Is it not true that when you cared, you entered the situation not only professionally but also emotionally?

These special ministerial experiences show us that we can be touched deeply and experience a certain intimacy with others. We do have a capacity to enter into deeper relationships and an ability to stay with such relationships no matter the cost. I can think of some of the marriage counseling that I have done. Week after week, for a long period of time, husband and wife continued to come. The sessions were very demanding. There was a growing intimacy. I was very deeply involved. Yet there seemed to be an energy that allowed me to continue with very little thought of the cost. I was entering into minis-

147

try with intimacy and it was calling me forth and supporting me.

When we do not face up to the challenge of intimacy in ministry, in friendship, and in prayer, we tend to give in to some rather self-defeating ways of dealing with this lack in our lives. For one, we may attempt to bury ourselves in our work or hide behind it. Or, rather than really face situations, we compulsively talk about them. Another escape is to get very involved in the social aspects of our lives, setting up a calendar that would weary the jet set. We can turn to alcohol, drugs, and "affairs" as a means of escaping from facing the genuine needs in our lives. This is all part of the human condition, to be looked at gently and compassionately. But if we don't look at them and see them as warning signs we will continue a pattern of behavior that in many ways blocks the activity of the Holy Spirit in our lives. "Nature abhors a vacuum." If we deprive ourselves of healthy, wholesome relationships in and through which the Holy Spirit can act in our lives, we will begin to fill the space with things that will be barriers to her love.

How do you react to a statement such as this: "When in the course of time, we acknowledged our friendship and recognized our ambition was a life of true wisdom, we became everything to each other: we shared the same lodging, the same table, the same desires, the same goals. Our love for each other grew daily warmer and deeper"? Could this be about two priests? What would you say to a priest who would speak this way? Could you see yourself saying this?

It was, in fact, written by a bishop, about himself and another bishop, both of whom are recognized as doctors of the Church. We celebrate the common feast of Saint Basil the Great and his friend Saint Gregory Nazianzen on January 2, a feast right at the beginning of the year that celebrates a friendship. This text is found in our office of readings. It is placed there expressing a model for us.

For us relationship is very much a part of the mystery of Church, of Christ and redemption, of incarnation and a God who becomes fully human — the blend of the human and the divine into oneness. We are human, very human. We are also divine, divinized through baptism, made partakers of the divine nature. There needs to be oneness within ourselves. And there needs to be oneness with others, certainly on the level of supernatural love but also on the human level. We are embodied spirits. Not a body and a soul somehow put together, but a unique whole, with body and spirit intimately one. The body is very much a part of our spiritual journey. As priests we are called to a celibate chastity. The United States Bishops' Committee on Priestly Life and Ministry reminded us that as celibate persons we should seek to establish bonds of permanent and steadfast friendship that will strengthen our capacity to forgo the exclusive friendship. Keeping it all together, human *and* divine, body *and* spirit, emotion *and* will, is not easy. Some experience it as a problem, others find it a challenge and a joy, while still others of us see it as a mess, even as something that it is better not to talk about. All of this is true — and more, it is the mystery of divine love in human form.

In today's society we are faced with attitudes concerning relationships and sexuality that are contrary to our traditions. We are also painfully aware of situations that have occurred in our country and which have forced us to face up to the serious psychosexual immaturity of some of our brother priests. These situations have seriously damaged the credibility of a celibate priesthood and have cost the Church dearly financially. As sexual human beings we must be relational, but we are to live our relationships with the necessary sexual dimension in accord with our celibacy for the kingdom. This is something very difficult in a world where sex is usually seen as synonymous with sexuality.

I will always be in debt to Donald Goergen for his insightful study of human relationships. Let us look at the levels of relationship that he sets forth.

First, there is the *acquaintance level*. Perhaps this

can best be expressed as the level where we are being friendly rather than being in a friendship. The characteristic of this relationship is that our exchanges keep exclusively to externals, like work or sports or just idle chitchat. We never go deeper. I like to refer to this as the "war stories" level; we get together and talk about what's going on in and around our lives, but never what's going on within ourselves. In itself this is perfectly good. It is a healthy social level. However, all too often priests take this for friendship, and it really is not that. And they never seek to go further into a relationship.

Goergen's second level is *friendship*. At this level there is a beginning of unity of spirit. Something new is being created. A trust is being built up that is supportive. Because of a greater openness, there arises within the relationship a genuine feeling of being helped and of helping. Friendship with all the dynamics that come to play within it is difficult to describe. It is something that is sensed and believed more than something that can be precisely defined. The poet can better capture it:

> Don't walk in front of me,
> I may not follow.
> Don't walk behind me,
> I may not lead.
> Walk beside me,
> and just be my friend.
> — Albert Camus

I am aware that a presentation of levels of relationship, logical and sequential as it is, doesn't correspond to our actual lived experience. In real-life situations we operate on all these levels at once. Also, I would like us to remember that these levels of relationship are applicable to a celibate priest's relationships with both women and men.

The next level of relationship in Goergen's schema is described as *intimacy*. Here we experience that comfortableness with a friend and he or she with us so that we are able to begin to disclose ourselves ever more intimately to each other. We listen with empathy as the disclosure takes place. We are ready and willing to be vulnerable. And we are not afraid of confronting each other on real basic issues. We are able to be honest and to express "tough love" with each other. Someone pointed out to me that this is the type of intimacy that should be present between two priests when they enter into the sacrament of reconciliation with each other. This is the kind of relationship Jesus had with his disciples.

From such friendship and intimacy there ordinarily develops a true sense of *affection*. This is an emotional response. Not the romantic emotion experienced by a couple and not a genital attraction, but an emotion that could be very sexual in the deeper meaning of that word. There is a drawing out of oneself, a deeper and more total commitment to the other person. Such an experience should not be something that unusual in our lives. I can remember a number of times when I have experienced a deep sense of loss because of the death of someone with whom I had developed a true friendship. I had a very special communion call that I made regularly over a long period of time. The bond that grew between us went beyond the ordinary priest-parishioner relationship. It was the relationship of two friends sharing the spiritual journey right to the end. It is sometimes only when the person is no longer there that we realize what a deep emotional bond has developed between us. On the more joyful side, there have been for me deep sharing of the journey to religious profession, ordination, and marriage — culminations that brought to the surface lots of real human emotion.

As one passes through these levels of relationship there is a natural movement toward oneness, toward surrender, toward the desires of cocreativity. This is most naturally fulfilled within a marital relationship where genital intercourse expresses total self-gift and a complete commitment to each other. For us as celibates genital activity is not where our relationships will find their culmination. We will cocreate something very beautiful, and that is the relationship itself with all the empowerment that flows from it, an empowerment that enables us to bring life to others.

This relationship that we create together will need to be carefully nurtured. All relationships have their season. There is the springtime, a time of newness and freshness, a time of excitement. New life is experienced, felt, believed in. We move on into summer when there is tranquillity and warmth, a season of quiet with a certain amount of activity, but in a more accepted and relaxed way. Then can come the fall when, all of a sudden, there are moments of tremendous brightness and happiness and joy, and at the same time a sense that something is dying. It is a phase that is hard to comprehend. In a long-standing relationship, it may have something to do with mid-life crisis or be similar to it. Then there can be winter, a coldness, a sense that the friendship is over. And it may be over if for some reason it has not been mutually nurtured. Or it may just be entering a period of dormancy in order to blossom forth again in an experience of springlike newness.

There are certain risks that we face as we enter into the deeper levels of relationship that evoke affection. Besides the possibility that they can ensnare the heart and threaten our freedom, they can also draw us toward a genital expression of affection. It is here that we experience our very human vulnerability. There can be tension and struggle, and we may even have to face some failures in this area. We can all remember those warnings against "particular friendships" that we heard in the seminary or novitiate. They may have been somewhat misguided and overly cautious, but at bottom they pointed to a very real danger. Because of these struggles and the tension that arise and even the normal dilemmas that might present themselves, there is a tendency on the part of some celibates to take refuge in flight, to run away from developing relationships, to close down and regress. We are tempted to think that the only reasons

152

we have these struggles or attractions is because we have allowed ourselves to feel affection. And we begin to argue: "I would never have felt affection if I hadn't allowed myself to experience intimacy. And I would never have experienced intimacy except that I allowed myself to have friendships. And I would never have allowed myself to get involved in friendships if I had been satisfied with just being friendly." We conclude it will be safer if we keep everyone at an acquaintance level and avoid friendship, intimacy, and affection. Then there will no longer be any problems. If we do decide to pursue this path, what usually happens is that even more serious problems are created. The emotions and loneliness can give rise to obsessions concerning the genital. Or we can become very truncated human beings, unable to relate in any meaningful way or even to respond with color and emotion to life's experiences. This has been called the "sterile celibate syndrome."

When we do remain open to friendship and are confronted with failures we can experience a certain disintegration — a coming apart takes place. There are two ways of responding to our failures: one is negative, the other positive. The experience of Judas was a negative disintegration. He betrayed his friendship with Jesus and went out and hung himself. He fell apart and decided to go all the way. In the experience of Peter we see a positive response to disintegration. He failed his friend Jesus in spite of all his previous protestations of loyalty. In his failure, though, he learned a lot about himself. He wept, he returned to the community, and when the opportunity was given to him, he ran to the Lord and opened his heart and recommitted himself. The experience of weakness and failure and sinfulness resulted in a positive gain for him. He attained an insight that affected the rest of his life, his pastoral care, and his teaching. In his memory he could continue to recall these experiences and build on them. Moments of vulnerability and the consequences that flow from them can lead us to recommit ourselves to fidelity and to see an ever deeper relationship.

In giving retreats I have had fun putting the levels of relationship together in a symbolic sandwich. We take a slice of bread — our basic humanity — and then we put on the cheese of friendship, the ham of intimacy, the lettuce and mayonnaise of affection, and in marriage, another piece of bread on top, capping and in some way closing off the relationship by a total self-gift, expressed in genital intercourse. As celibates, we have, as it were, an open-faced sandwich, wide open, always open to more cheese and ham and mayonnaise — more friendships, each with its own proper intimacy and affection. If I decide that I don't want to take the risks of friendship, intimacy, and affection, and want to stay with just the acquaintance level, then there would be no cheese and ham, no mayonnaise and lettuce in my life, only bread, and we know that man does not live on bread alone. It makes for a pretty meager diet, a very dry one.

You may be having the same reaction that I get on retreats. Yet, because of the homeyness of the analogy, don't miss the depths of what we are talking about.

Often I have been asked how we can bring the proper discernment to the particular relationships in our lives. I'd like to respond to this question in a general way and in a specific way. In general, I have found it helpful to examine relationships in the light of three negative qualities: competitive, addictive, and exploitative.

Competitive: Is this relationship competing with my call, my commitments? Is my presence in the other person's life competing with her or his call and commitments? If it is, then this needs to be looked at. If it isn't, then I can move on to the next.

Addictive: Because of this relationship, do I find myself frequently distracted, drawn away from my responsibilities and my duty? Does this relationship prevent me from living according to my proper lifestyle? If it does, it has to be looked at. If it doesn't, I can look at the final negative quality.

Exploitative: Is this relationship truly leading to growth — socially, physically, emotionally, intellectually, spiritually — for both of us? Or are we exploiting each other? Are we inordinately attached to each other and using each other? If the relationship is exploitative, this has to be looked at.

If our relationship is noncompetitive, nonaddictive, and nonexploitative, then it will probably be a real asset to our life and ministry. It will be a positive part of our spiritual journey. If any one of these negative qualities is present, then the relationship definitely needs to be further examined. It need not necessarily be terminated. The greater challenge, leading to significant growth, might lie in freeing it of the negative quality (or qualities).

Let us explore things a little more deeply now and specifically by considering some aspects of relationship proper to celibates.

First of all, there has to be fidelity to the celibate commitment on the part of both persons involved in the relationship. Even if the other party is not committed to celibacy he or she must share with us our commitment to celibacy for the kingdom. That person must also be true to his or her commitment and we must share in that responsibility. It is natural that affection will grow between two persons who begin to share intimacy. Such affection will inevitably lead to certain questions and even temptations. And since we are human, we may well make some errors of judgment. We need to maintain a strong conviction that the genital has no proper place in our relationships as men committed to celibacy. Genitality does not offer us an appropriate means to express affection. To bring the genital into our relationship will destroy either the authenticity of the relationship or our commitment to celibacy for the kingdom.

We also need to be on our guard against exclusive relationships. Our ministry demands we be free and open to relate with many people. At the same time, to demand or even allow someone to center her or his life on us, while we can only give our friend divided attention because of our priestly commitments, is unfair and will necessarily become problematic. When two persons engage in a mutually exclusive relationship that cannot express itself in the normal way and come to a creative fulfillment the relationship often becomes "cannibalistic" — the friends begin eating away at each other.

A real safeguard for us is to keep our relationships as public as possible. If we don't want people to know that someone is our friend, that is a real danger signal. There should be a willingness to share our intimate friends with the others with whom we are friendly. The more a relationship is hidden away behind closed doors, the greater is the danger that it will generate a negative energy that will eat away at the positive values that are to be found in the relationship.

Duration itself is not a problem. A genuine relationship that has been allowed to develop to the point of intimacy or even just friendship engenders a commitment to each other. Of itself, such a commitment is eternal. The relationship, unless it is violated, will last for the rest of our lives, in spite of long periods of separation because of transfer, change of assignment, and the like.

We need to be on our watch when there is a significant age difference. If there is a great age span, we might question whether the friendship really is that of equals. There may be another dynamic coming into play that may prevent both parties from acting as fully mature adults in the relationship.

When a relationship is playing a significant role in our lives, it is important that there should be a third person in on it — a third person with whom we can discuss the relationship. Ordinarily this will be the person we are relying on to guide us in our spiritual journey, the one we sometimes call spiritual director. The guidance we are receiving cannot be complete or integral if we withhold the presence of a significant relationship in our lives. However, there may be special reasons why in a certain case we feel we cannot talk to our guide about a particular relationship or the relationship may be with the guide. Then we need to turn to someone else, perhaps a very close friend. The important thing is that there be someone there to help us objectify what is going on in the relationship and to help us keep our balance if the emotions threaten to become overwhelming. We need help to discern whether the course the relationship is taking is wise or foolish, whether a particular relationship is really contributing to our growth or actually dissipating our energies. No one is a good judge in his own case.

Finally, as men committed to Christ in celibacy for the kingdom, all our other relationships have to be held in the context of our primary personal commitment to friendship and intimacy with Christ Jesus. Not only should no relationship be allowed to interfere with our prayer relation with Christ-God but our relationships should be brought to prayer. It almost flows from the very nature of who we are that any intimate relationship we have will have to include sharing our relationship with Christ, sharing prayer. Christ will be a part of any authentic relationship we have as priests. I find this to be so, even when the friendship is with a Jew or a nonbeliever.

Relationships should never be taken lightly. They are serious business. I was made to realize how serious they are for celibates on a retreat I conducted for religious women. One of the religious present on that retreat was going through a genuine process of grieving. A very good priest-friend of hers had died after a long illness. And the sister did not know to whom she could turn to express the depth of her sorrow and find understanding. There were few, she felt, who could understand how two celibates could love so deeply and yet be wholly faithful to their commitments. We should grieve deeply at the death of an intimate friend. See Jesus weeping at Lazarus's tomb. If there has been a third person with whom we have been sharing the relationship, she or he will be there in our hour of mourning and grief. We need a companion when our spiritual journey is marked with such grief.

The perils that accompany intimacy — important as intimacy is — for us celibates point once again to the importance of developing support groups, especially with our brother priests. Here we can find the support and affirmation, the spiritual accompaniment we need. We do have a responsibility to walk with one another on the spiritual journey. The Holy Father recently led a retreat for priests in France. In the course of it he expressed this desire: "I wish also that a true fraternity may unite you, deeper than all the differences, a fraternity that is sacramental and that also exists on the level of feelings." We need this support, this affirmation. We need a place where the many questions relating to our relationships can be discussed with one another in confidence. We need a place that is confidential. A place where we can talk with one another knowing that what we share will not enter into the stream of gossip.

There is one thing that really undermines the relationships that exist among us priests and holds us back from becoming intimate and finding the strength and support that intimacy can give us. And that is the insidious tendency that exists among us to gossip about one another, to cut one another down. In the course of years in priest personnel work I sadly noted that if a man achieved some success, that success was talked of once; but if he had a failure, that was reviewed over and over again. One of the joys of my ministry in priest personnel work was in seeing men given a second chance, in seeing men given a chance to take leadership positions in spite of the fact that some had boxed them in as being failures. A perhaps heroic but eminently practical expression our fraternal love can take is to adopt resolutely the decision that all gossip will stop with me. And, if possible, it will be turned around into affirmation.

We have talked about a lot of things in this chapter. Many of them bear wider application. I hope the one thing that has gotten across is the vital importance of true friendship in our lives as celibates — despite the danger and cost. I don't like to hear priests say: "I have many, many friends." It indicates that they do not understand what true friendship involves and probably do not have a single true friend. No one has the emotional energy to have many, many friends. We should have the energy to have many, many acquaintances, to be friendly with many people. It is part of our ministry. We are blessed if we have the time and energy to enjoy and profit by the gift of two or three true friends.

In one of the dioceses I visited, there was a discussion concerning how priests used their time off and the tensions that arise because of the expectations that are brought to bear upon this. The discussion made me aware of a need we want to address. A priest has basically three areas of responsibility in his life: his ministry, his diocese or religious community, and himself, that is, his health, his mental and emotional well-being, his spiritual growth and ongoing renewal. It seems that in the broader Church-community there is an understanding of the responsibility of priests to their ministry and to their diocese or community and, of course, to the Church. But there doesn't seem to be an understanding of his responsibility to himself. One of the services that we can render one another is to be willing not only to educate ourselves concerning these needs but also to educate our people. They need to see the value of these needs being cared for in our lives and the value of us priests having relationships in our lives. When I was first ordained, my pastor, whom I came to love very much, told me it was his practice never to go to a parishioner's home for dinner for fear that others would talk. He felt that if we went to dinner with one, we would have to go to dinner with all the parishioners. In the light of this wisdom, for the next two years, I turned down every dinner invitation. Then another associate arrived. He didn't buy the pastor's practice. Following his example I soon discovered the joy and the learning experience that dinner with parishioners offered.

We need to develop relationships at all the different levels. If some want to be critical of us, then that is part of the price we have to pay to build life-giving relationships into our ministry. If this were the only price we had to pay for something so enriching, we would be getting off very cheap.

In the *Christopher News Notes* of April, 1979, I came upon this prayer that I have used on all my priest retreats. It seems to me to be a good way to conclude our consideration of friendship:

God, why is it so hard to get close to people, to let people get close to me, to make friends? Is it because I've been hurt before and am afraid to be vulnerable again? Is it because I think others will take advantage of my openness? Your Son had twelve close friends; one sold him for thirty pieces of silver, another denied that he even knew him, the rest ran away when he needed them most. Jesus even predicted these things, yet he did not shut himself off from friendship. Make me willing to take the risk too. Help me to realize that ultimately in opening to another human being, we are opening ourselves to you. Amen.

9

Celibacy for
the Kingdom

I must admit that I am personally inclined to favor the adoption of optional celibacy for the diocesan priest, even though I have seen the sociological and economic problems this causes among Eastern priests of the Orthodox and Catholic communions. (Obviously, celibacy for the kingdom is an essential element of monastic life and religious life as we now know it — though societies of married priests professing obedience and evangelical poverty are a possible form of religious life. The Second Vatican Council did encourage the development of new forms of religious life, and such a possibility as this does not seem to be excluded.)

It may be an option that will be forced upon us. In this regard I would like to quote a priest who, in my opinion, is one of the most eminent and respected theologians of our time, Karl Rahner: ''It cannot be denied that the right of the community to have a sacramentally ordained leader takes precedence over the efforts of the Church (which certainly deserves respect) to have community leaders who accept the obligations of celibacy. No one can claim with certainty that, for all times and for all cultural groups, the association of priesthood, in the unity of its governing and cultic functions with an academic training and celibacy, will be and will remain feasible to a sufficiently large extent. If this were not so, the Church ought to have pressed long ago for celibacy in the Eastern churches and to have said that here, too, a sufficiently large number of celibate clergy would be possible."

The eminent theologian draws the interesting parallel between the action of Pope Saint Pius X in reducing the requirements for receiving the sacrament of the Eucharist with what another pope might do in regard to the eucharistic priesthood.

Rahner considers the question from the side of ministry, which is certainly right. But I think it also needs to be considered from the side of vocation. Is enough respect being given to that to which God is calling men (and women)? Or might not Jesus say today: "You set aside the call of God in order to follow the traditions of men." The dual call to marriage and ordained ministry is being respected in the case of Anglicans and Lutherans coming into communion with Rome, but at the present time there seems to be no room allowed to consider the possibility of such a call in the case of men who have labored all their lives in fidelity within the Roman communion. It seems strange that the dual vocation of men like Eddie Doherty and Charlie McCarthy has been respected in the Eastern Catholic Church but not in the Western Church in which they had been reared. The outspoken unwillingness with which some priests live celibacy obscures the witness of all celibates to the detriment of the Church and community. But it is not easy for these men to see God's manifest will in the law of celibacy when their own inner sense is that God is calling them otherwise.

Yet I have to admit that I am challenged by the words of the Second Vatican Council in regard to the consonance of celibacy with the ministerial priesthood. After exhorting married priests "to persevere in their holy vocation and continue to devote their lives fully and generously to the flock entrusted to them" the Council, in the *Decree on the Ministry and Life of Priests* (No. 16), goes on to say:

> There are many ways in which celibacy is in harmony with the priesthood. For the whole mission of the priest is dedicated to the service of the new humanity which Christ, the victor over death, raises up in the world through his Spirit and which is born "not of blood nor of the will of the flesh nor of the will of man, but of God" (Jn 1:13). By preserving virginity or celibacy for the sake of the kingdom of heaven priests are consecrated in a new and excellent way to Christ. They more readily cling to him with undivided heart and dedicate themselves more freely in him and through him to the service of God and of . . . [the human family]. They are less encumbered in their service of his kingdom and of the task of heavenly regeneration. In this way they become better fitted for a broader acceptance of fatherhood in Christ.
>
> By means of celibacy, then, priests profess publicly their willingness to be dedicated with undivided loyalty to the task entrusted to them, namely that of espousing the faithful to one husband and presenting them as a chaste virgin to Christ. They recall that mystical marriage, established by God and destined to be fully revealed in the future, by which the Church holds Christ as her only spouse. Moreover they are made a living sign of that world to come, already present through faith and charity, a world in which the children of the resurrection shall neither be married nor take wives.

These words merit some serious reflection. Some of us might not readily identify with some of the lofty imagery used, especially when we have known the day-to-day gritty struggle with sexuality that celibacy can involve, although there are some rich veins of truth running through this reasoning.

However, no matter what might be our personal position in regard to optional celibacy for the diocesan priest and no matter how much we find ourselves in agreement or disagreement with the theological reasons set forth in behalf of the fittingness of a law of celibacy, the fact remains that almost every man called to ordination to the ministerial priesthood in the Latin rite is obligated to embrace celibacy for the kingdom. Therefore, each of us, with this value as with all values, needs personally, as it were, to corner himself and appropriate the values here with mind and heart. We have to strive to see what it really is and make it our own and commit ourselves to it.

Some, today, question the very possibility of a person committing himself to anything or anyone, especially in a permanent way. This does not do justice to the dignity of the human person. We belong to God by virtue of creation. He has total rights over us. He has, though, given us ourselves. He has given us freedom. And he respects that freedom as no one else does. He who knows us through and through, knows that this is the most important thing we have because herein lies our power to love. And God is love.

God has given us ourselves and by that gift we are in turn free to give ourselves, and free to give ourselves in a permanent way. Even in such giving, our freedom remains with us. We can take back what we have given. And sometimes we should. The power of dispensation within the Church is God-given and is used in his name. It has its place and this should be acknowledged. To remain faithful is an ongoing gift. We must daily, hourly, receive the gift and confirm it in our lives.

We can give ourselves and commit ourselves to celibacy, to celibate chastity. In our God-given freedom we can control, direct, restrain, and redirect our life energies with the help of his grace. To say that we can't, or to believe that we can't, or to act as though we can't, undermines our very humanity. The difference between a human person and an animal lies in such freedom. The animal, unless physically restrained, has to follow its impulses, its attractions, its instinct.

It is good for us to realize that we are, as they say, rational animals. We do have an animal part to us. This part of us responds automatically. And it is an integral part of who we are. We do have feelings, emotions, and attractions as well as thoughts that arise spontaneously. Because we are sexual persons with bodies made for sexual expression, we will have sexual feelings, emotions, and attractions. These are good, natural, and healthy. If I am a normal, healthy person, and I see a beautiful man or woman with openness, I will experience an attraction. If I, seeing as a human person, see that person as a human person, the attraction won't be wholly nor primarily on the physical level, but physical attraction will be there.

This is all good, and it is to be acknowledged as good if we are going to be healthy and balanced. The precisely human reality is that I can recognize and acknowledge this and then I can decide what I am going to do with the attraction, feeling, or desire.

The attraction to other persons extends to our own gender. And it is still good. Other men are attractive to men. We all have our homosexual side. It may be more or less developed; it may or may not be dominant. Be that as it may, for a man, deep union and communion with other men with that fullness of human relation which in some way involves the body — but in a nongenital way — is good and natural. Part of our problem in the area of sexuality comes from or is heightened by the way we have restricted the physical. Every human relation — save a very pure transcendental union with God — if it is truly human, has its proper physical expression. The fuller, more open, and complete the relation, the fuller, more open, and complete the appropriate physical expression. Obviously there has to be a fidelity to true humanity, a real reverence for each other, and realistic awareness of the danger of selfishness, of using the other, of unintegrated passion or lust betraying us. This is certainly obvious in our present-day society. Perhaps not so obvious is the fact that we priests have as great or a greater need of support and encouragement to be human and accept and use the due physical expressions of love and friendship in our friendships with both sexes. A certain fullness and satisfaction in this area is perhaps the best safeguard against lust.

Even in masturbation we do need to acknowledge that there are human goods and values present. This is why it is attractive to us as humans. It is a satisfying (in a passing way), tension-releasing experience. Masturbation can put us in touch with the goodness and power of our physical being, something of the wonder of our human body. Yet it has to be honestly acknowledged that such an expression of our sexuality falls short. It is only an aspect of a possible fuller human act on the physical side; the communion of love is not present. Sin is the choice of a good — for the human chooses only what he perceives as good — which lacks some of its due goodness. In sinning, we sell ourselves short, choosing something that does not have all that it ought to have for us. This is why it offends our loving heavenly Father. He does not want to see us sell ourselves short and settle for less than the fullness he has intended for us.

When we discuss things like this, things that touch the depths of our humanity, we are always talking in a somewhat desiccated or abstract way. In every human act there are so many levels of actuality. Whatever be the goodness in any physical act we place, in any feelings we have, it can be vitiated by a lack of integration, integrity, and completeness.

The fully human lies precisely in our free decision as to what we are going to do with our natural and good feelings, attractions, and desires. This is true whether we are committed to celibacy or not, whether we are heterosexual, homosexual, or bisexual. Our commitment and our sexual orientation do not change our basic humanity and our responsibility to respect ourselves and our humanity and to act humanly. Celibacy as a human commitment, albeit enlightened and empowered by grace, lies first of all in human decision, not in the physical or at the level of feelings, attractions, and desires.

It is possible to embrace a sort of celibacy for reasons that have nothing to do with faith or God. But I do not want to spend time here exploring such a possibility or the motivations that might lead to that. We are men of faith. The just person lives by faith. Anything we do without faith is for us "sinful," that is, it falls short of being worthy and true to us as to who we actually are: men baptized into Christ, divinized, transformed, brought to a new level of being. In this, what we are physically, humanly, is in no way left behind. All of this is to be fully integrated and lived, for it is fully part of who we are.

However, our humanity, and to our point, that important dimension of our humanity, our sexuality, can be integrated in different ways. The question of vocational discernment is precisely this: "How can I personally best integrate the richness of all that God has given me? What way will best support and facilitate my living in the greatest fullness of my true being as a Christed, divinized human person?"

God has been too generous. We have more potentials than we can ever hope to use fully. We must choose to give scope to some while leaving others relatively dormant, at least for certain periods. We can commit ourselves — we have the freedom to do this and want to come to the level of being able to exercise that freedom — to seek to develop fully certain of our gifts or potentialities and to lay others aside.

One of the greatest and most profoundly beautiful potentialities of the human person is to grow in love through intimate communion with another, sacramentalizing or making present in sign and in reality the communion of love that God-Christ has for his created ones. To prepare carefully and well to exercise such a potentiality so as not to desecrate it is only being humanly responsible. To commit oneself to live for a lifetime such a potentiality is courageous, bordering on the heroic. Because of the reality inevitably sacramentalized in the enactment of this potentiality by divine disposition clearly revealed to the Christian, such an enactment can be worthily expressed only in the context of an enduring commitment. God's love for us is faultlessly enduring. The sacrament of it, to be worthy of what it sacramentalizes, must also be faultlessly enduring.

To exclude permanently from our life the possibility of bringing into actuality such a sublime potency not only calls for a most careful consideration and preparation but also the implementation of other potentialities of comparable beauty and sublimity, or the commitment is foolish and unworthy of us.

Thus we come to the question of the why of celibacy. What are the values within celibacy that make it worth forgoing the sublimity of a committed love that sacramentalizes in a way that which effectively fosters the growth of love, human and divine, in ourselves and in the lives of others? Celibacy must at least do something equal to this for us.

Celibacy for the kingdom does.

However, just as marriage, raised to a sacramental level in the revelation of the new covenant of Christ-love, while it is in divine intention such a sublime reality, in particular persons it will be this only if the human person sees, understands, integrates, and lives the reality, so too celibacy for the kingdom will be such a reality — one worthy of forgoing other potentialities — only if we understand, integrate, and live it.

Every analogy in some way limps, though analogy is often a good way to convey an idea or impression with more impact or feeling. The way celibacy was spoken about when I was in the seminary gave me the sense of a man who was going to the altar to be married and all he was thinking about was all the women he was giving up without any thought to the one he was about to marry. In choosing a partner in marriage a man does, in a very real sense, give up every other possible partner. It certainly is not good if this is the way one primarily sees things. Indeed, it is important that the committed do still allow time and space for other friendships. But the partner does have primacy, a claim on prime time and attention.

Indeed, if the relationship is going to be what it should be, each will want to give as much time and attention as possible to the other, for they have decided that this is where their happiness lies.

All of us want happiness. But what is happiness? Where is it to be found? As I have said before, happiness is found in knowing what we want and then knowing we have it or are on the way to getting it. It involves a real choice.

If a relationship is going to work and bring happiness, it is necessary to make the choice that it is precisely in this relationship, in growing with this person that I am going to find my happiness. It is necessary to choose the other, warts and all, to love the other with his or her weaknesses and not in spite of the weaknesses. In loving someone with his or her weaknesses we are living up to who we are, for we are the image of God and this is the way he loves all of us. As humans, we naturally love the good that is there. God loves the good that is not there and thus causes it to be there. Loving partners each create the partner in fullness. The lacks are a source of growth for both.

Celibacy for the kingdom is fundamentally a choice, a way to happiness, and a choice of a partner, namely God-Christ. It is a positive choice. It is the decision that I will find the central love of my life in the Lord. I will give my relationship with him primacy — a primacy of time and attention. For us to grow to the full, there has to be a central, committed, permanent love in our life. If we have only partial loves, uncommitted loves, not totally demanding loves, then we will never grow to our full potential as lovers. And this is what essentially we are, for God is love and we are made in his image.

As celibates we are invited to choose God as the central, grounding love of our lives and to give primacy of time and attention to him and to our relationship not because we have to but because we choose to. In choosing this and in living it we will find our happiness because we will have what we want.

We choose this relationship with all its warts. Not that there are any warts in God in himself, but in our experience of him. He is mysterious; we cannot fully understand him. He is known in faith; he is not a palpable presence. But let us not delude ourselves: every human lover is also mysterious and is absent at times. Fidelity in any love commitment is going to demand all a human person has and more — God's grace.

There are going to be times of loneliness — physical loneliness and the deeper loneliness of being faithful to the absent lover. There are going to be other attractions. What partner who remains open, lively, and loving, is not at times drawn to another? It is at these times that choice is reaffirmed, deepened, and breaks through to new depths of communion.

Do you remember that delightful tale of the Little Prince? He lavishes much care on his special rose and comes to love it very much. And the wise one points out to him that the more he gives, sacrificing for what he loves, the more he loves and finds joy in the other.

Essentially, celibacy for the kingdom is the choice to have God-Christ as the primary, basic, committed love relation in our lives, all other loves being fuller and richer in coming out of this love where we learn to truly love. Indeed, all loves are in this love, for all are one in Christ. This is why celibacy frees us to be so fully to others. In loving Christ we are loving them. In loving them we are loving Christ, who said, "Whatever you do to the least you do to me" (see Matthew 25:40).

We may make this choice of celibacy because at some moment God revealed to us his lovableness and we knew he was the one we wanted, that no one else could ever make us happy the way he can. We may make it because we have become aware that any human partnership would be for us truncating or at least could be truncating — that it would be impossible or almost impossible for us to find another human person who would go all the way with us or who would give us the freedom to develop fully the magnificence God has made us. We may have wanted the greater freedom to be with a Lover with whom we could be to all whether in formal ordained ministry or in the ministry of everyday Christian life and being. Or we may make this choice very much in faith: it is required of us, it is the only way we can make sense of our life, the only way to be a wholehearted lover, to be fully human.

The important thing is choice and commitment. Realistic choice — the choice of reality — free, knowledgeable choice. We know the Church clearly recognizes that marriage and vows and commitment to celibacy, when made without freedom, without the necessary understanding and knowledge, are not a choice, are not a reality. The choice cannot exclude the warts; the whole reality must be chosen or it is not truly chosen — a selective choice can never lead to true happiness.

There must be commitment — living the choice to the full and steadfastly — or the full growth and maturation of love and life can never be attained. This is not something that happens overnight. We grow into it, with the help of God's grace and the support of our brothers and sisters, our hearts being purified by successive challenges, by falls as well as by victories.

What are some of the consequences of the choice and commitment of celibacy for the kingdom — the choice of Christ-God as *the* partner of our lives?

It is here perhaps where we encounter our difficulties.

A struggle all men have: we have to make time for our Lover. He is always with us and we do all with him and for him, so it is perhaps easier for us celibates to rationalize ourselves out of love time, especially since a presence in faith is not usually so tangible as a human partner. Yet this love relationship, as much as any, needs times when we let everything else go and just be with the Beloved. A celibate lover has a special need for a contemplative type of prayer. This is so not only because it is where we will most fully experience our Lover and our Lover's love for us, but also because it is important for

171

our own maturation and integration. Most men, in marriage, will have a woman to help them come to terms with and integrate their feminine side. Celibates can have some very good friendships with women but never such a lifelong intimate presence as is provided by a wife. We want to grow as much as we can through the relationships we have with women. But it will be with the openness, the gentleness, and the receptivity of contemplative prayer that our feminine side will most fully emerge. It will be encountered as beautiful and friendly, and it will be integrated. Through encounter with our femininity, our masculinity becomes more developed and pronounced. Without such an encounter we are apt to be less virile, even effeminate, in touch only with a superficial femininity. If we do not have a sufficient grasp of our masculinity, we may fear the emergence of the feminine. This may be why some of us are afraid of opening to a contemplative type of prayer. In turn, this lack of the contemplative dimension in our lives may account for why some of us priests are rather effeminate or react to life's situations in a rather womanish or unmanly way or conversely have to put up a macho façade.

Another challenge arises in that our Beloved has such an intense and complete love for everyone else and invites us to be with him in this love that it is difficult for us humans to be that universal. We experience different degrees of attraction and repugnance and when the attraction is present it is difficult for us to moderate our love and keep it fully in context.

In celibacy the physical seems to have little place in our central love, though we should perhaps look at this more closely. Contemplative experience can at times be intensely sensual. In any case, we might do well to bring the body more into our communion with the Lord and enjoy more the expressions of his love for us in the magnificence of our bodies and the rich experience of the sensations of his creation; in other words, to be aware of all the caresses of his love in all good feelings — especially in the embrace of a brother or sister; the odor of his love in every good smell; the savor of his love in every good taste; the sound of his love in all the rhythms of life. If we are more in touch with the presence of his love in all that is human we can more fully, freely, and openly enjoy the expressions of his love in all the intimacies of our friendships. We will not fear the touch and feel of human love but rather be nourished in our celibate love by such love grounded in our central love. Our society has been plagued by a sort of "hands off" or "go to bed" attitude. When there is reverence and true love grounded in a central love, it is possible to enter into very full and satisfying physical expressions of our relationship without using the other, exploiting the genital, or going beyond what is appropriate to the relationship in the context of our commitments.

As celibates, like any human who has not stifled the fire of his humanity, we will have to moderate our very real and God-given passion and be watchful of the deceits of lust, for we all do have the seven capital sins well rooted in us. But true love, grounded in and one with our Beloved's love with its reverence and care for each one loved, will be our greatest safeguard against the exploitations of lust.

Nonetheless, we are sinners. We do fail. We have our failures in other areas of our priestly lives: anger, sloth, gluttony, drink. . . . We may have our failures in this area also. Because such failures frequently involve another person they are compounded and can become very complex. Insofar as we ourselves are concerned, we need to handle such failures with the same realism as we would the other failures in our priestly lives: first, honestly face up to the failure; second, forgive ourselves and seek and accept the forgiveness of God and of the others who have been hurt; third, make practical, realistic resolutions to guard ourselves as much as possible against repetition of our failure; and fourth, do our best to live these resolutions. When other persons are involved, we need to seek to do full justice to them for the pain and harm and burden we have brought into their lives. Complete honesty with them in regard to our commitments and our resolutions will greatly help heal the situation and prevent its repetition.

A truly celibate life — a celibacy for the kingdom — is a life filled with love, with all the joys and sorrows that love brings. It is a happy life, for we have truly chosen what our life is all about: the center of our love is Christ-God — we always have what we want. We and our Beloved are together and one in a way no other partnership can attain. The feelings of loneliness and the sense of absence, however much they press, will be seen as challenges to a more persistent choice and commitment.

Each of us has to come to grips with the basic questions of choice, commitment, self-mastery and gift, intimacy and physicality. I have tried to share here something of the way I have come to see things — not without some real struggle and failure, a seemingly long journey — and I can witness now that it is an understanding and a way of loving that has brought me more happiness and a sense of fulfillment than I suspected ever possible. For all this I acknowledge the giftedness and thank the Lord.

Of one thing I am sure, there cannot long be a vacuum in our lives. Soon enough it will be filled up — if not with God, then with another person or perhaps with a dog or some other pet (to what extent does that dehumanize our ability to love?) or maybe alcohol or drugs. A psychologist pointed out to me another love substitute that is taking hold of all too many: television. It is a rather insidious lover that seems to have a great potential to ensnare. It would be well for all of us to check on how much of our time this "lover" might be demanding. How much of a hold has TV on us now? Try doing without it for a bit and see. It is possible to get the news from the radio or a newspaper. If there is a television set in your own room, take it out (what excuses come up for you when you think of that?) and use only the common set in the house. It's worth ensuring our freedom.

Probably some of us have never fallen in love, or if we have, we have forgotten what it is like or have tried to forget (the memories can be painful) and do not relate that experience with the present love of our lives. The idea of speaking of God-Christ as a Beloved, of having a love affair with God, etc., may sound kind of flowery to many of us. But look at the Scriptures. How does God describe the relation he wants with us? The passion of the Song of Songs has its message.

Recently I received one of those new electronic watches with a half dozen control buttons. Fortunately, it came with a book of instructions. It was a job, but I finally got some idea how it all works and it seems to be serving me well. I could have thrown out the rather complicated little book of instructions and decided I would figure things out on my own — and still be figuring things out from now till eternity. We are like that with that somewhat more complex thing called our lives. The Lord has given us a guidebook. But instead of taking the Scriptures seriously and working with them to figure out how to make our lives work, we leave the instruction of the Scriptures aside and try to figure things out for ourselves — and wonder why we get in such messes! God made us. He knows the way we work, the way we attain what we want: happiness. We need to take him seriously in this.

We are told God made us to know, love, and serve him. Do we really believe this? Do we construct some unnatural kind of love we are supposed to have for God that leaves out happiness? Do we construct some kind of false distinction between natural and supernatural? That beautiful and holy Father of the Church Henri de Lubac was sent into exile a decade before the Second Vatican Council for suggesting we make too much of this distinction. His wisdom prevailed at the Council and was acknowledged with a cardinal's hat. All is from God. It is all beyond our worth, our deserts. Trying to distinguish too sharply between the natural and the supernatural tends to lead to a sort of Pelagianism in practice. We begin to act as though there was a natural sphere which we can handle by ourselves. The Lord has been rather explicit: "Without me you can do *nothing*" — not even the so-called natural. The distinction also leads to our regarding those things that we relegate to the supernatural as being things about which we can do nothing — so we put-put along waiting for God to do everything. We do not take the responsibility that is ours. All is grace, and grace is given in all that is. We are by creation the very image of God. Without the divine dimension of life we cannot be fully human. When we leave the divine dimension out, we are not natural, we are unnatural.

Let us take God seriously and listen to what he says to us in the Scriptures. Let us open to such love, to such a Lover:

> You are my friends.
> The Father and I will come and make our dwelling with you.
> If one opens I will come in and sup with him, side by side.
> I have loved you with an everlasting love.
> I hold you in the palm of my hand.
> Does a woman forget her baby at her breast, or fail to cherish the son of her womb? Yet even these forget, I will never forget you.
> You will sit with me on my throne, just as I sit with my Father on his throne.

For cultivation of any love relationship two things are necessary: time and space.

We know from our counseling how essential it is that a love relation consistently be given time, personal time. It is necessary to waste time with each other.

Have you ever run into this case? The marriage is coming apart and the couple come to the priest. The husband proclaims he cannot see why she is unhappy. He then details all the things he is doing for her, all the good things he is making possible for her: he works three jobs; she has her winters in Florida and summers in Maine, her furs and jewels and cars. . . . What more could she want? Why is she unhappy? When he has finally run out of breath, a meek little voice speaks up: "But if only he would give me. himself once in a while." I sometimes think God looks down from the balcony of heaven at his very busy priests, busy doing wonderful things for him, and says: "If only they would give me themselves once in a while."

There is, in fact, nothing you or I can do for God that someone else cannot do — in fact, I think most of us hard workers will be spending time in purgatory for doing things that God wanted to do himself or have someone else do — except one thing. There is one thing that we can do for God that no one else can ever do. If we don't do it for him, he is just out of luck, he just can't have it. I might even say that from all eternity God dreamed of the day he would bring us into existence just so he could have this. That one thing we can do for God that no one else ever can do is to *give him our personal love*. If we do not give him this, no one else can ever give it to him. It is the one thing he wants from us. Everything else follows from it: "He who has my commandments and keeps them, he it is who loves me" (John 14:21). If we love him, we will do whatever else he wants. But all our doings without this love mean nothing.

Like every lover, God wants some of our time just for himself. This is hard for us to believe: that almighty God wants my love, my time, my attention. After all, he is God. I can do things for him. That makes sense. But my just spending time enjoying him in love — how could that make any difference to him?

There is a pericope in Saint John's Gospel that those in the early Church and Saint John with them evidently considered an important part of the Good News. This is evident from the fact that John repeats the story; though it is prominent in the synoptics, he has placed it in a very prominent position in his Gospel, just before the final paschal events, and he insists on the presence of the risen Lazarus, Jesus' greatest miracle presaging his own resurrection. Moreover, Matthew has Jesus declare: "Truly, I say to you, wherever this gospel is preached in the

Let it be told again to us: "Six days before the Passover, Jesus went to Bethany, where Lazarus was, whom he had raised from the dead. There they made him a supper; Martha served, and Lazarus was one of those at table with him. Mary took a pound of costly ointment of pure nard and anointed the feet of Jesus and wiped his feet with her hair; and the house was filled with the fragrance of the ointment. But Judas Iscariot, one of his disciples (he who was to betray him), said, 'Why was this ointment not sold for three hundred denarii and given to the poor?' This he said, not that he cared for the poor but because he was a thief, and as he had the money box he used to take what was put in it. Jesus said, 'Let her alone, let her keep it for the day of my burial. The poor you always have with you, but you do not always have me' " (John 12:1-8).

I think our first instinct on hearing this narrative is apt to put us right there with Judas, despite all John's "uncharitableness" about the man. Why this waste? When we sit in silent prayer, that word of Scripture tends to assail us: Why this waste? There is so much more I could be doing with my time. There are so many needs — the poor in spirit, the poor in body. Why waste time sitting here in silence before the Lord? I could be out there working for and with the Lord. (In fact, we won't be very much "for and with the Lord" out there if we don't spend some time sitting with him within.) We wonder about the prodigality of fracturing an alabaster jar and pouring out thousands of dollars' worth of perfume.

The Master speaks. He who expressed such love and care for the woman at his feet when she came to him in Simon's house has not changed. "Leave her alone. She has done a good thing." Jesus-God does want us to waste on him: time, money, our talents. Certainly, he was not unmindful of the poor. The poor knew that best. No rabbi had ever so identified with the marginated: born in a stable, rushed into exile, a poor hard-working carpenter from "Hicksville," the son of a widow. He first blessed shepherds and later invited fishermen and tax collectors to be his intimate and chosen friends. He touched lepers! — as well as the blind and the crippled and others afflicted with every sort of disease. He fed the hungry. He is indeed the Master of the poor and outcast. Yet, as the poor so well know, there is a time and place for prodigality. He, the Holy One, had intimately accepted the love of a prostitute. Could she ever be too extravagant in the expression of her love? Never.

Jesus wants our extravagant love; he wants us to pour out on him personally something of the richness of the life he has given us.

The fragrance of what Mary did filled the whole house, lifting all there to new levels of experience. The intimate communion of contemplative love is a leaven in Jesus' house, the Church, and in his world. A contemplative dimension is meant to make each one's life more fragrant in giving witness to the divinity and humanity of Christ — the Anointed One — our God.

Jesus speaks here the Good News. We want to listen to it with the greatest of care so that its goodness can permeate and inform every aspect of our own lives. One of the questions that came up for me, as I listened to the Scripture we have in hand, is this: "Where did Mary get this fabulous jar of perfume?" Lazarus was a good brother and quite well-to-do, but I wonder if he was that well-to-do and that wonderful. It more likely was something that the exotic woman of the streets might have bought to lure customers. Or the pay of some merchant prince, enamored by the beauty of the woman of the streets who pleased him so well. If that be the case, what does it tell us about Jesus? That he would accept such a gift? It says to me, that no matter what has been our track record, no matter how much sin has been woven into our lives, he still wants us to pour out our lives' love on him. He does not withdraw himself from intimate and loving contact with sinners. Rather, when we come to embrace him in heartfelt prayer, he proclaims to all: "She has done a good thing."

Maybe you never did have that initial experience of love with the Lord, when it seemed you could never spend too much time with him. If you did, go back to it in memory, the deepest part of one's soul, and relive it. Let it come alive again and live out of it. Give him now a chance to show you such love again.

It is necessary for us all to make time for love, for love of the Lord.

And space. Some priests have been relentlessly faithful in making time for prayer, but they have never allowed the space for prayer. "Relentless" is the right word for what they have done. They have worked at it, made it a task, a real labor, and not always a labor of love. Others have given up. After all, Jesus had said: "Come to me, all who labor and are heavy laden, and I will give you rest [— not burden you]" (Matthew 11:28). If my prayer is such a burden, they reasoned, this is not what the Lord wants for me.

Just before he left for the Orient on what was to prove to be his final journey, Thomas Merton met with a group in California to talk about prayer. With his usual enthusiasm and vehemence he cried: "The best way to pray is: STOP. Let prayer pray within you, whether you know it or not." He added: "It's a risky thing to pray, and the danger is that our very prayers get between God and us. The great thing in prayer is not to pray, but to go directly to God. If saying your prayers is an obstacle to prayer, cut it out. Let Jesus pray. Thank God Jesus is praying. Forget yourself. Enter into the prayer of Jesus. Let him pray in you."

We need to learn to relax, relax with a Friend — just to be open and waste time with him. Centering Prayer is a good way to begin to get into this kind of space. Other possibilities include walks through the park or country, taking a leisurely ride, listening to poetry or music, or just quietly sipping a cup of coffee — in short, set aside some spacious time for love on a regular basis. If you are reacting negatively to such an idea . . . well, do you really want a life without poetry, music, love? Have you given up on yourself? *God hasn't!* He is an incurable romantic. Give him and yourself a chance; make some time and space for love.

If you were looking for someone to help you find the meaning of your life, who would you turn to? Would you go to someone who is obviously happy in love, joyful, eager to share, outgoing and loving? Or to one who is resolutely duty-bound, marching to orders? Or to someone whose life seems to be going nowhere, giving no evidence of vision, no evidence of being en route?

How do people see you? Alive in love? Resolutely dutiful? Going nowhere? (If you don't know, try to open some space to get some honest feedback. The young are especially helpful in their frankness.) How would you like people to see you? Do you want it enough to do something about it?

We can certainly stand straight and tall, for we are the sons of God — like unto his Firstborn; indeed, one with him. We can choose to restrain our genitality and avoid any binding relationships in order to be free as the Son of the Father to be to all the children of the Father in friendship and caring love. We need periodically to recommit ourselves to Christ in celibacy: "Even now do you not call me, 'My father,' you who are the bridegroom of my youth?" (Jeremiah 3:4).

I once attended a special two-weekend program geared toward a certain transformation of consciousness. Prior to the first weekend there was a meeting of the participants and the ground rules were laid out. We were all asked to make a commitment to observe the rules during the two weekends. There were enough of them and they were quite demanding, but fair, and they were called for by the process involved. Whenever during the course of the program one or another of us messed up and failed to observe one of the rules, the leader confronted us directly and with firmness. He did so by simply asking: "How can you respect yourself if you do not live up to your own commitments?" The answer is obvious. We can never have any real self-respect if we do not at least strive to live up to that to which we have committed ourselves. Nor will anyone else respect us. Celibacy for the kingdom is a very precious commitment. If we see it for what it truly is — an invitation to a very special and intimate love relationship with God himself — we can hardly overestimate its sublimity, no matter how messy it might seem to get in the daily struggle to live it.

Before ending this chapter I want to say something about homosexuality. It is a reality among us. There is no reason to doubt the statistics that say that at least ten percent of the population is gay. It is not unreasonable to accept the contention that the percentage is probably higher among us priests and religious. Those who serve frequently as confessors and advisers to priests and religious sometimes set the percentage a good bit higher. Celibacy is the one unquestioned path for the devout Catholic homosexual.

Yet many of us priests do have our prejudices.

A few years ago I had occasion to take part in a *cursillo*. It was a wonderful experience. If you have not had an opportunity to participate in one yet, I would certainly encourage you to do so. It is like being submerged in a sea of love in which the great and ever present current is the Lord himself. In the course of the three-day program some fifteen brief talks are given, mostly by lay persons who make up the support team.

One of the talks is entitled "The Obstacles to Grace." On the occasion of my *cursillo* this talk was given by Brother Tom, a real Friar Tuck type: fat, jovial, full of the joy of the Lord, a man known for his compassion — he runs a shelter for the homeless in his city. I was very surprised by Tom's talk — and I think most others were, too. But it was a good surprise.

Tom told of the day of the pope's visit to Boston. He and his community all donned clean white habits and boarded two buses early in the morning for the two-hour ride to Boston Commons. Tom is a bit of an operator and so he had gotten a special ticket. While the rest of the brothers went off to join the ranks of the many religious already there, Tom sailed up the center aisle. Suddenly a group broke out applauding the figure in white. Tom waved joyfully as the placards went up: PROTESTANTS FOR THE POPE. As he advanced, another crowd broke into applause. Tom began to respond as their placards went up: GAYS FOR THE POPE. Quickly his hand came down and he looked hurriedly in another direction.

The day turned foul and a deluge came down, trying to dampen the spirits of an ever enthusiastic mob. Finally, the Holy Father departed, the lights went out, and the crowd began to disperse. Tom had gone about six steps when suddenly he realized he had lost one of his shoes in the deep mud. He groped around for it as people surged past him until finally he was the only one left on the muddy field, himself as muddy as the field. Two young men came along and asked, "Can we help you, Father?" Usually Tom is quick to let people know he is not "Father," but that night he needed all the help he could get. He gratefully accepted. The search proved fruitless and was finally given up.

Now Tom had another problem. Where were his buses? He had no idea, though he knew the names on the street signs where they had parked. The young men offered to guide him. Well, it was like with Mary and Joseph in Jerusalem: When Tom and his new friends got to the corner, both buses were gone, each presuming Tom was on the other. What to do now? Lowell was two hours away and it was very late. The cheerful young men offered to drive Tom home. At first he protested but gave in with a sigh of relief.

As they drove off, the driver said, "Father, we saw you coming in this morning and we all cheered for you." "Oh! You're the 'Protestants for the Pope'!" "No. We're the 'Gays for the Pope.' " Oh, boy! Here he was to arrive home very late, covered with mud, one shoe on and one shoe off and *two gays in tow*. As they reached the monastery Tom knew he had to invite the men in for a cup of coffee, though he secretly hoped they would decline.

However, still their cheery selves, they were quick to accept his offer.

As they sipped their coffee the men told Tom that their gay support group met each Monday evening in the basement of the church across from the Boston Gardens for prayer and sharing. Wouldn't he come to join them Monday? Tom looked at his calendar and gratefully reported that he had a *cursillo* meeting. The next week? No, a committee meeting. The following week? Caught!

Three weeks later, Tom quietly slipped into the basement of the old church, hoping no one had noticed him as he did. The group stood around in a circle, quietly praying, singing from time to time. Suddenly the young man standing next to Tom broke out in deep retching sobs. Forgetting everything, Tom took the lad into his arms and held him close. As he listened — "No one loves me, no one accepts me, not even my own family will accept me" — Tom recalled that morning's Gospel about the leper whom Jesus had reached out to. And the Lord created a new heart in his servant.

As Tom finished his story, there were tears in more than one pair of eyes. Father Joe, the chaplain for the course, spoke up: "God keeps pushing our edges," he said. "I just discovered that there is a Moonie on our *cursillo*. I remember what Lincoln once said: 'I don't like that man. I have to get to know him better.' I am going to invite our Moonie brother and some of his friends to come over to my house for dinner next week."

We all have our prejudices. It is good if we can recognize them; better if we can do something about getting rid of them — like getting to know our brother. If we don't know any friend as a gay, it might tell us something about how prejudiced we are, or at least seem to be to our gay brothers, that not one has ever "come out" (as the expression is) to us. I am afraid we have all been at priestly gatherings where gays have been the butt of our stories, little mindful of the fact that there are gay brothers among us who have to mask their real selves and join in the laughter, even as they are pierced through and through and made to feel even greater isolation where they had come for brotherhood and support. If ever we are tempted to make a derisive remark about homosexuals, let us reflect that we are talking about our brothers, perhaps our pastor or our bishop. We are certainly talking about Jesus, for our gay brother has been baptized into Christ. "Whatever you do to the least, you do to me." We may not be able to understand a homosexual orientation — especially if we have never made the space to have a real honest talk with a gay brother about sexuality — but we do need to respect all and respect all the ways in which God is leading others. Any priest who has had any amount of ministry to gays can witness to how powerfully God's grace is working in some of their lives, especially in the face of the present scourge of AIDS (Acquired Immune Deficiency Syndrome). There is a compassion abroad that comes straight from the heart of Christ. Why is it that in some the homosexual side dominates? The answers, with varying degrees, are many. The fact remains that in God's providence a good many are going to have to find their way as Christ's gay disciples. They may well identify more easily than their straight brothers with John who rested his head on the Master's bosom and knew his intimate embrace. They certainly have as much right to be respected as any other priest or Christian as they follow the Lord in discipleship.

There is some resentment toward gay priests by their straight brothers because the message is sometimes conveyed that the gay is not bound by celibacy in the same way as the straight. Such resentment, I think, is quite legitimate. If we have made a commitment to celibacy, it makes little difference whether we are gay or straight. The Church, and by Church I mean each and every one of us, has every right to expect that we will live up to our commitment. In individual cases, the struggles, the weaknesses, and the temptations can be greater and can provide excusing factors. It is not for us to judge a brother but to support him in compassion. Yet a gay does little for his own dignity to claim his basic orientation as a general excusing factor. If he is a normal healthy person, he is as free and as responsible as any heterosexual person. There is a lot of woundedness in the homosexual community. Understandably so. To grow up with the realization that you are generally rejected by society, faced with great prejudice within your Church and oftentimes not even accepted by your own family, in many ways forced to live a double life — it is something of a miracle if you are not seriously marred by so much negativity.

A man who has managed to stay healthy and whole in the face of all of this is usually an exceptionally healthy, selfless, and giving person, and that is what we often find in our gay priests. It is difficult for a priest who has not had the experience to sense fully what a gay priest suffers as he gives himself wholeheartedly to the service of his people, always with the realization that if they find out he is gay many of those whom he is serving so tirelessly will reject him out of hand no matter how much he has done for them and their loved ones. Add to this the rejection he fears from his fellow priests and his bishop. It takes an exceptional love of Christ and of others, a special purity of heart, to continue in such ministry. Every priest worthy of the heart of Christ should want to make his brother's heart lighter by shunning all prejudice and being as open to the gay person as he is to the straight. We are all the sons of the Father, one in the Son. Together we all face the challenge of being celibate lovers, of living in a way that gives clear witness to that kingdom of love for which we embrace our celibate way.

10

Mary: Our Life, Our Sweetness, and Our Hope

We had just finished supper at the English villa by Lake Albano in Italy. Some of us began to clear off the table. I noticed there were only three of us doing this; the rest of the priests had left. Next thing I knew, someone poked his head through the door of the dining room and said, "Come on, you guys, for the *Salve*." There they were, nineteen priests from England and Ireland standing before the statue of the Blessed Virgin Mary, waiting for us three priests, three Yanks, to join them in the singing of the *Salve Regina*. Singing the *Salve Regina* after meals is a part of their tradition.

Devotion to the Blessed Virgin has been quite strong among us priests. Mary was presented to us as the "lady" in our lives. And yet, in leading priests' retreats, I have become aware that our devotion to Mary has changed quite a bit. This change is a reflection of the times.

It is obvious to me that faith in Mary, the Mother of God, is still as strong as ever among us. Our faith in Mary is based on the reality that the ultimate purpose of our devotion to her is to glorify God and to help us to commit ourselves to a life that is in absolute conformity with his will. In these two regards, giving glory to God and comforming to the will of God, Mary is for us a model.

With the faith still so strong, why has there been such a shift in the way we express our devotion to Mary? There are a number of things that come to mind: the propagation of popular devotions that are not theologically and liturgically sound; the attraction of some of the faithful to Mary as holder of secrets; and the use of devotion to the Blessed Virgin by some of the more "traditional" groups as a sign and symbol of "orthodoxy." How many of us have had to deal with people who will judge our worth by our adherence to a particular devotion or apparition of the Blessed Virgin Mary? Our non-adherence has led to our being condemned with the stinging reproof: "And you call yourself a priest!" Of course, for every one of these painful instances, there are many more joyful and enriching experiences that we can cherish.

The times — as well as what is going on among our people, and our own reactions — challenge us as priests to reflect on our faith-response to the mystery of Mary and reevaluate our devotional practice. It would be a real loss for us and for those we serve if Mary does not have her rightful place in their lives.

Pope Paul VI in *Marialis cultus* gives us the basic norm for evaluating true devotion to Mary: "The only worship that is rightly called Christian takes its origin and effectiveness from Christ, finds its complete expression in Christ, and leads through Christ in the Spirit to the Father."

There are four basic dogmas concerning Mary that ground my response to her and help me keep balance in this area. Let me briefly set them forth:

First, there is the reality that *the Blessed Virgin is truly the Mother of God.* This young woman really conceived and gave birth to God himself. She said "yes" to an awesome vocation. She became God's Mother according to his human nature. Jesus, her child, both God and man, rested comfortably in her womb, experiencing the gentle beat of her heart, feeding off of her nourishment, and sensing her slightest movement. Often he kicked and moved about, causing Mary to take Joseph's hand and put it on her abdomen to let him feel the stirring of life within her. This was the beginning of a journey for Mary as the mother of a very exceptional child. As a good mother she journeyed with him every step of the way. All of Mary's other privileges and titles flow from this fact of faith that she is truly the Mother of God. The new liturgical feast of the Mother of God, which we celebrate on January first, summons us to reflect on this sublime motherhood. On the liturgical feasts of Mary, I think it is important that we do devote some time reflecting on the relevant scriptural readings and the readings from the Fathers. The fruits of tradition are rich. I find that such reflection adds a deeper dimension to the words I speak of Mary, the Mother of God.

Have you gotten into discussions about *the perpetual virginity of Mary?* There are some strong feelings and beliefs among Catholics and non-Catholics alike in regard to this. Our belief in the perpetual virginity of Mary is a tradition that goes back to the third century. But the full significance of it is still being explored. It is a belief filled with reverence for the child she bore, but it is not altogether clear what that reverence demanded in regard to Mary's experience in giving birth to her Son. In a class I attended recently, one of the students challenged the professor when he said that it may be possible that Mary experienced the normal pains of childbirth as Jesus came forth. The objector argued that pain is the result of sin, therefore Mary never experienced pain. The professor's response was obvious: "If this argument be true, then somewhere in the course of her life Mary must have sinned, for at the foot of the cross the Father allowed her to experience great pain as she watched her Son suffocate to death." Whatever else it means, Mary's virginity does not mean that she did not know the full experience of motherhood. Rather it gave her an exceptional freedom to enter into that experience and live it fully. This is something of what our virginity or celibacy means for us: a freedom to enter more fully into the experiences of life, and especially that of spiritual paternity-maternity, bringing Christ forth in our own lives and in the lives of others.

It is easy for us to present poor theology about Mary if we do not keep listening to the Scriptures, the teaching of the Church, and good theologians. Take the *Immaculate Conception*. We must not lose sight of the fact that Mary had to be redeemed like the rest of us even though she was preserved free from original sin. Her little child was not only her son, he was also her redeemer. It is fascinating, this unique relationship between mother and son. In Mary we see the full extent to which the grace of Christ can heal us, to the point where Adam's sin will no longer leave its mark upon us.

The fullness of Mary's victory over the consequences of sin is made manifest in the *Assumption* event. Mary, after her life on earth, was assumed body and soul to the glory of heaven. The Church has never defined whether or not Mary died. Did Jesus let his mother experience death so that she, too, could be like us in all things but sin? We do not know for certain. But we do know that he took her to himself, body and soul, as a complete human person. How important our human nature is to Jesus — not only in his coming to us, but in our going back to him! If we deny any part of our integral humanity, we deny something of his special gift.

In these four dogmas, the divine maternity, the perpetual virginity, the Immaculate Conception, and the Assumption, I have found the theological foundation for my devotion to Mary.

Pope Paul VI was painfully aware that a growing disenchantment with devotion to the Blessed Virgin was spreading within the Church. This continues. There are those who think her way of seeing things is too restrictive and her lived experiences too special or particular to have any application to the vast spheres of activity open to humankind today. Some feel that she is just something added, apart from the fundamental forces at work for our salvation. Others have placed her in such a position that it seems to rival Jesus' role as redeemer. If we have allowed such sentiments as these to influence us, then we might find that our devotion to Mary is not all it used to be. However, Mary's influence in the lives of Christians, far from being something restrictive, adds depth and sensitivity. Her role in salvation is not something secondary. She is at the very heart of the saving mysteries and constantly helps and teaches us.

Is it any wonder that Pope John Paul II in January, 1987, announced the Marian Year and reaffirmed it by the encyclical letter "Mother of the Redeemer"? It is hoped that the Marian Year will promote an authentic and more committed celebration of the Virgin Mary. The purpose of the year is to prepare the Church, and through the Church, the whole world, for the celebration of the bimillennium of the birth of Jesus Christ. Let me share with you some thoughts about Mary that have affected my life and ministry over the course of the years.

Mary's Role in the Mystery of Christ and the Church

At the Second Vatican Council, after much discussion and a close vote, it was decided not to have a special statement on the Blessed Virgin Mary, but to integrate the Council's teaching on her into its total consideration of the Church. There is an important message for us right in the title of the section on Mary in the *Dogmatic Constitution on the Church*. The title of the chapter is: "The Role of the Blessed Virgin Mary, Mother of God, in the Mystery of Christ and the Church." The Fathers of the Council would not allow Mary to be placed in an isolated position. ~~Belief and~~ devotion to the Blessed Mother make no sense unless they are founded on the mystery of Christ and the mystery of the Church. If the Blessed Virgin Mary's role as Mother of God makes no sense unless it is founded on the mystery of Christ and the Church, is it not also true that our role as priests makes no sense unless it is founded on the mystery of Christ and his Church? Context is so important and integration so essential for both Mary and for us as priests.

It seems to me that the difficulty in understanding Mary and her place in our lives arises when we allow ourselves to be distanced from the Gospel portrayal of Mary and the doctrinal teaching that has been laboriously drawn from that portrayal and made more explicit through the slow and continuous process of the living tradition. It is up to each age to receive the fullness of our Christian heritage and to enter deeply into contemplation of the Blessed Virgin Mary in order to discover how that age can best express its devotion in ways compatible with the times. Mary's wholehearted "yes" to God needs always to be there but lived in different ways.

Marian Dogma and Social Justice

A very significant development in the life of the Church has taken place as a result of the proclamation of the dogma of the Immaculate Conception and that of the Assumption. This was the first time that dogmas were proclaimed in the modern era without using the ordinary process. The ordinary procedure would have been to wait until there was a theological consensus on the dogmas, flowing from the work of theologians. In the case of these definitions, the popes rather listened to what the Spirit was saying to the People of God. They consulted with the bishops of the world who in turn were asked to consult with the faithful in their areas. From the clear witness to the sense of the faithful that emerged, it was obvious that belief in the Immaculate Conception and the Assumption was part of the living tradition of the Church. Therefore, these events of salvation history were proclaimed dogmas of the Christian faith.

There has been a shift on the part of the magisterium to listening to the people, listening to their hearts, listening to humanity. In this listening, a deeper, fuller, and richer meaning of the human vocation has been perceived, as it had been worked out by God in Mary. In her Immaculate Conception, human nature in her experienced a healing; in her Assumption, human nature was fully restored and glorified, completely and permanently integrated in itself and in the divine plan. With the clear perception and definition of these two dogmas, in a sense, there was no place to go further in the development of doctrine concerning Mary herself.

Since the proclamation of the Immaculate Conception in 1854 and, even more so, since 1950 and the proclamation of the Assumption, there has been in the Church's public pronouncements more extensive expression of a genuine concern for the temporal aspects of life within the world.

For example, there has been a greater involvement in setting forth and safeguarding the value and sanctity of life; statements concerning labor, human rights, marriage and family life, abortion, birth control, economics, war and peace, and government have abounded up until the present time. Since 1891 there have been more major pronouncements, at least nine, dealing with world issues coming from the papacy. At the same time many of the national conferences of bishops have also issued pastoral letters dealing with these issues.

Some have felt that there has been an overemphasis on Mary in the century embraced by the definitions of the two dogmas. On the other hand, many lament the rapid decline of Marian emphasis since the definition of the Assumption. But I think this is all providential.

What we are all meant to be has been understood with a new clarity as it is seen exemplified in Mary. The Church understands more and more clearly the dignity and integrity to which every human is called. At the

~~same time the more attentive listening to the faithful~~ aroused a new awareness of how sin was affecting the social order, doing violence to humanity, degrading God's children. Hence, the mounting concern with social issues, a search for the ways to bring Christ's healing and integration to all of humanity as it has already been brought to the Blessed Virgin Mary in her Immaculate Conception and Assumption.

Perhaps we priests have not entered into this new listening as well or as fully as have some of our people and many of our bishops. In a recent talk for priests, Father Richard Rohr took the words of Jesus and applied them to the social issues of our day. The fruit of his own prayer and deep reflection, his applications were concise, clear, and penetrating. They caused something of an uproar among the priests present: "Who does he think he is questioning our American way, the value of the capitalistic system, the upward climb of the middle class, the need to make our country impregnable, our generosity as a nation, the enjoyment of hard-earned profits, the all-out fight against communism, and so on? I could never go into my pulpit and speak like that; the people would never stand for it. Who do you think pays the bills around here?" I found myself personally very challenged. I had to go to the Lord and ask the Spirit to help me discern how much of what I was hearing was indeed the authentic call of Jesus and how much might be the interpretation of Father Richard Rohr. What is Jesus saying to us today as those responsible to carry through on the teaching of the Council, of our recent popes, of our American bishops, in their application of the Gospel to our American way of life?

When we stop to think of it a bit, it should not surprise us that a deeper entering into the mystery of Mary should lead us to a deeper social sense, to an active concern for social justice. After all, it was as one of the poor that she dared to proclaim before the entrenched leaders of her own society and nation this program for a new social order:

He has shown strength with his arm,
he has scattered the proud in the imagination of their
    hearts,
he has put down the mighty from their thrones,
and exalted those of lowly degree;
he has filled the hungry with good things,
and the rich he has sent empty away.
— Luke 1:51-53

The Anima and Animus

Carl Jung's theories are well known and effectively influencing the life journey of many today. For him the successful spiritual journey is a blending and balancing of the *anima* and the *animus*, the passive and the active. The male unconscious embraces the female aspect, the *anima*, the passive, the receptive and relational, the compassionate, the gentle and caring. The male conscious, the *animus*, is the active, the powerful, the effective, dominating by reason and control. It needs to bring forth and integrate the feminine, the *anima*, into its consciousness.

In our ministry, is it not true that our people are looking for something of the *anima* characteristics in our response to them? These characteristics are happily more present in the Church today, even among the clergy. Here, we can see the influence of Mary and her modeling — at Cana and elsewhere in the Scriptures. We have all reflected on the drama of Jesus' first miracle and Mary's activity on that occasion. She was the attentive one, first to perceive the situation that would cause so much embarrassment to their hosts, the celebrating couple, and their families. She entered into their plight and felt it as her own. Then she acted in the most effective way she could to respond to the need: she approached her Son. She put her awareness and feeling into effective action.

The spiritual journey is concerned with receptivity to the Spirit. " 'What no eye has seen, nor ear heard, nor the heart of man conceived, what God has prepared for those who love him,' God has revealed to us through the Spirit" (1 Corinthians 2:9-10). A complete receptivity has both a passive and an active dimension to it. We have to be passive enough to allow what is unfolding around us to come into our experience and bring to us the message of what God is allowing to happen in our life situation. We also need to be vigorous in acting according to what the Lord is calling us to through this perception.

Our sisters are helping us here also. I had occasion to work with one of our prominent archbishops a few years ago. Recently I had the opportunity to attend a diocesan gathering at which his presentation was enthusiastically received by the priests and people. I marveled at the difference in the way he approached things, in the caring way he was to people. I was told that since I last worked with him he had had the occasion to work very closely with women religious, something he had never done previously. They had had a great influence on him and on the way he now lived his ministry. They helped him get in touch with his *anima*.

A recent report prepared for a priests' senate explored men and women working together in ministry. It highlighted the differences and indicated something of what we can learn from one another and how we can work better together, complementing one another in respect. We can serve both men and women better, if we are aware of the *anima* and *animus* characteristics. Listen: "While both men and women in this sample are concerned with relationship, women seem to value a more personal relationship and deeper sharing. Men seem to place the job to be done as a priority in working with women and feel the need to maintain more distance. In decision-making, women seem to be more concerned with the process and men with the outcome. Women seem to expect men to recognize that they are burdened, and men feel this expectation as pressure for them to take on more work. Many of the areas of tension between men and women throughout our society arise from stereotypes that each sex has of the other."

I have found working with women — and bringing my experience back to reflection in the light of Mary, letting the modern behavioral sciences contribute their insights — has enabled me to open to a whole other side of my personality and to bring it more and more effectively into my collaborative labors with women and into my ministry as a whole. In this sense, perhaps, most truly I can sing in the *Salve* that Mary is my life written big in her modeling and the source of my sweetness, a real hope for continued growth and integration.

Mary and Ecumenism

Mary is a topic we often try to avoid in our ecumenical conversations with our Protestant brothers and sisters. Yet I have found that in looking together at Mary, some of our basic differences have been clarified. I, too, have found that some Protestants have a biblical appreciation of Mary that throws light on my perception of her. Recently, I found a Protestant who said that Mary is blessed in three ways: first, blessed in that transformation of human nature, which is the gift of the Spirit in each one of us; second, blessed in her openness to God's words, a modeling that can assist each of us in our openness in accepting and proclaiming the Word of God; and third, blessed as our particular friend, a fellow disciple of Christ, ready to help us on our journey. A really inspired understanding of Mary, one that sums up much of what I have been endeavoring to share in this book.

Mary the Disciple — A Life of Faith and Fidelity

Pope John Paul II pointed out, in one of his Holy Thursday addresses to priests, that there is in our ministerial priesthood a special likeness to the Mother of God. At ordination, "by the anointing of the Holy Spirit, we are marked with a special character" and are "so configured to Christ, the priest, that we can act in the person of Christ the Head." Ours is a calling to be special coworkers with Christ. Is that not like the calling Mary received, that bonded her to the saving work of her Son? John, the beloved disciple of Christ, who heard the words "Do this in memory of me" and became Christ's priest, the next day heard Jesus say to his mother, "Behold your son." Mary is our spiritual mother, entering into our lives as we express our *fiat*, surrendering to the Father's will. Mary is our mother, modeling perfectly for us the imitation of Christ her Son and our Lord — a perfect model of discipleship.

A disciple is one who so loves that his or her life is one of faith and fidelity.

The Second Vatican Council spoke of Mary's life as "a pilgrimage of faith." She gave her consent in faith, and her life as mother was lived in faith. We easily forget this, that Mary had to live by faith. Faith allowed her to trust completely in God's providence, although she could not fully understand his plan. Living a life of faith is not easy; it always involves suffering. Simeon told Mary, "Your own soul a sword shall pierce." We tend to want to live a life free from pain and suffering; we like to live our lives on our own terms. We can dissipate a lot of energy resenting our restlessness and pain. Far better is it to follow Mary's example and patiently accept all our pain and confusion and live a life of faith and trust. The choice is ours.

Mary freely accepted the journey of faith when she made that great leap of faith and said her *fiat*. She had her questions: "I am a virgin; how then can this be?" Yet in the end she responded: "Behold the handmaid of the Lord, be it done unto me according to your word." (See Luke 1:34-38.) Her *fiat* was heroic, but it did not exempt her from continuing to live an ordinary human life. She experienced the cares and hardships of daily existence, the daily routine of making ends meet, the death of her husband, the role of the widow, the pain of a mother over an only child's departure from home. Her Son even reminded her that her greatness was not in her role as his mother, but rather, as with everyone else, in hearing and accepting the word of God. Recall that scene when Mary was standing in the crowd and a woman cried out, "Blessed is the womb that bore you and the breasts that nursed you." What did Jesus' reply — "Blessed rather are they who hear the word of God and keep it" (see Luke 11:27-28) — say to Mary's maternal heart?

Father Schillebeeckx' comment on all of this was, "Her example of faith shows us how faith in the mystery of the living God is stronger than human life, stronger than even death, even the death of her own Messiah."

Our greatness does not lie in our role as priests, but in the depths of our faith and the transformation which that faith brings about in us. Only in faith can we believe and accept the fact that the mystery of Jesus is the foundation of the life and the mission of the Church and of our priesthood. Jesus is at the center of it all. How important it is then for us constantly to renew our faith!

We need constantly to renew our faith in the Church as the sacrament of saving unity: "Where two or three are gathered in my name, there am I in the midst of them" (Matthew 18:20). It is comparatively easy to see our Lord's presence in faith-filled, small-group communities. But, at times, it is very difficult to see his presence in the institutional Church, which is the overall structure uniting these faith-filled communities. Our faith and faithfulness as priests can grow only if we are able to see the presence of Christ in the institutional Church. For some of us there is a need to make peace with this Church.

Sometimes I get too entangled in the events of the present moment. When I do, I fail to see things in their total context. When things are not seen in their total context, we lose the wisdom of faith. Let me share with you a passage from my journal. It was a renewing occasion, one where I saw things in context. This was written during a visit to Rome in 1986.

I walked into Saint Peter's Square. Oh, how slowly I walked along in the square, going up the center, right into Saint Peter's. I found myself looking over my right shoulder to the pope's apartment and I remembered the time we celebrated the Eucharist in his private chapel. He is what he is. His approach is a gift that comes from his background. He has never known a Church that exists in a free society, and therefore his gift is that he wants to protect the Church. I thought of what an unbelievable schedule he has. I'm amazed and in awe of his ability to speak so many different languages and of his deep concern for the many different parts of the Church. Lord, I need to pray more for him and forgive him for being all too human. So many different men have lived in that apartment. As one elderly priest once asked me: "What is more important, the papacy or the pope?"

I continued my walk toward Saint Peter's. I noticed the many pilgrims from so many parts of the world. This reminded me of just how universal the Church is — which sometimes in the United States I forget. And then into Saint Peter's. This time a slow walk, clockwise, to just look again, to drink it all in, to say *arrivederci*. I passed the low modern relief of Pope John XXIII. I appreciate more now how radical and courageous he was to start the whole Vatican II process and to empower in the bishops of the world the determination not to make the documents of the Council just a restatement, but rather a powerful proclamation of faith. I passed one of the priests who is living with me in this clergy house. He is a Scripture scholar, dedicated to his work. He was on his way to class, having just finished hearing confessions in three different languages. Once again, I was attracted by the mosaics. They are so powerfully present all over Rome. Here, in the art of Saint Peter's, millions of little pieces, each different, are drawn together to present a total picture — a symbol of what the Church universal is. And the marvelous works of marble! Today I was especially aware of the work over one of the doorways. In front of a pope there is the arm of a skeleton holding an hourglass to remind us of time, and death, and resurrection.

I paused a moment at the altar of Mary, *Mater Ecclesiae*, and I realized how I have a deeper appreciation of devotion to Mary through my return to the study of theology. As I approached the Chair of Peter, I had to pause and look at the four great doctors of the Church holding up that chair. I realized that I really need to do my share of holding up, defending, and supporting the Chair of Peter. I prayed that I would be what I need to be in this area: always true. True loyalty is conscientious in speaking out on issues that are important and need to be talked about. In many ways, it is part of our tradition in the United States to feel the freedom to do that and yet at the same time to be loyal. I turned and looked again at the main altar. My mind went back to the tour of the *scavi* and the reality of the tomb of Saint Peter below the main altar. I recalled that Saint Peter's is a church that has stood unmoved in one place, but has had many foundations and stages of growth in its history. I wondered if someday some pope will decide to build over the foundations of the present Saint Peter's because it will be thought too small and inadequate. The passage of Sacred Scripture came to my mind, "Peter, you are rock and upon this rock I will build my Church." This is Jesus' Church, it is the way he wanted to ensure that his message would be to all ages. I am a son of that Church; I belong. It has a profound role in the history of the world. The Church and the papacy, signs for all times.

I continued my walk and I passed the chapel of the Blessed Sacrament. I paused a moment. I could see the monstrance with the Blessed Sacrament through a slight crack in the curtain. I became aware of God's presence in the Church, and a scrip-

201

tural passage came to my mind: "I will be with you all days, even to the end of the world." It is funny. I did not pause to make a visit, rather Christ visited me. Was it by chance that I stopped at an angle that allowed me to see through the crack in the curtain? Or was it a reminder to me of the mystery of Christ's presence in the Church and in the papacy? And then, as if to remind me that this presence is enfleshed and is genuine and real, I came to Michelangelo's Pietà: Mary, so youthful-looking, with Jesus in her arms. I cannot recall in what direction she was looking, whether at him or at me; it did not matter. It spoke to me of the cost of all that I had seen and thought in my walk through Saint Peter's. It said to me: "I mean everything that I have said and if you have any doubts, look at me and look at my mother."

As I walked again to the center of the basilica and looked down that majestic main aisle the workmen were taking away the chairs that had been set up for a special Mass for the students of the pontifical colleges of Rome, which was celebrated the night before. The awareness of the presence of God is found in the middle of the daily routine of life. I paused and leaned against one of the barriers and sincerely rededicated myself to the Church and to the papacy as a sign of God's presence in the world, and to the cost of it all — Mary, Jesus, and the Cross, the Spirit behind the visible. The Holy Spirit had truly surprised me. What started out to be just one last visit to Saint Peter's before I left Rome had ended up being a walk of faith and recommitment. I came out into the daylight, a bright sunny morning in December. I slowly walked across the square aware of the gift of Rome to the Church, but also, heading back home, of the gift the United States can mutually give to Rome. As I got into my bus to head back to the center of the city I found myself pondering all these things in my heart.

Not only are we and Mary disciples together in the pilgrimage of faith, we are also disciples together in the pilgrimage of fidelity. "You should think of us as Christ's servants who have been put in charge of God's secret truths. The one thing required of such a servant is that he be faithful to his master." (See 1 Corinthians 4:1-2.)

What is fidelity? To be trustworthy and faithful and in this to be rooted in love and in strong belief; to be committed as Saint Peter was, even though he was very much aware of his weakness; to be faithful as Jesus was in doing always the will of his Father. Fidelity is the capacity to commit oneself to the concrete partnership with God and in that commitment to develop the strength to abide by the commitment even though it may call us to make significant sacrifices. When we are committed, we have a determination to persevere. We dare not only to be responsible, but also to dream. We know that as the years go on we will be making adjustments in our commitment because of our desire to enter more deeply into it.

Mary practiced the virtue of fidelity. Her commitment underwent a considerable evolution during her lifetime. She was open to the word of God even before the angel appeared to her. She was committed to practice the piety that she knew of at the time; she was committed to the laws of her people and the elders. She learned to listen to the word of God. She was faithful to the traditions; she pondered them in her heart. She reflected on the events and circumstances of her life. These patterns were present in her life even before the angel came. She is a model for us in our practice of the virtue of fidelity.

Jesus has said to us: "You are my friends if you do what I command you. No longer do I call you servants, for the servant does not know what his master is doing; but I have called you friends, for all that I have heard from my Father I have made known to you. You did not choose me, but I chose you and appointed you that you should go and bear fruit and that your fruit should abide;

so that whatever you ask the Father in my name, he may give it to you" (John 15:14-16).

We remember this call; we have freely responded to it. This is the first aspect of fidelity: *I must freely choose*. We did freely choose. On the day of ordination we stepped forward and said "yes" to having been chosen. We wished to be faithful to the commitment, our commitment as priests and our commitment to the mission of being priests in a particular place. By being responsible for what we have promised, we freely choose to be signs of credibility, of honesty, and of caring. Our ordination day was a special day. We opened ourselves to the word of God.

Mary not only was open to the word of God but also was open to radical changes in her commitment. Imagine, after having committed herself to virginity in openness to the word of God as she understood it, along come those words of the angel. They deeply disturbed her. The outside God came inside; the transcendent God became imminent within her. God made a very special claim on her life.

Mary was not the only one to experience a call to such a radical change. What about Saint Peter? As John tells us in Chapter 21 of his Gospel, Jesus asked Peter: "Do you love me more than these others do?" and Peter said, "Yes." Three times Jesus asked him that question, and in asking he also asked him to tend his sheep. Peter was given a new role.

After our initial commitment at ordination, we enter into a second element of fidelity. It is not enough to make a free choice once and expect the energy of that decision to carry us through to the end. It is absolutely necessary that *our decision be reaffirmed*, because it changes, not in essence but in the circumstances of each day. Oh, it would be wonderful if each day we could get out of bed and say, "Here I am, Lord, your man — a Christian, a priest, and I am ready, willing, and able to leap into my activities of the day." It usually doesn't happen that way. Our commitment must be reaffirmed through the events of the day, through the words and circumstances where we hear the voice of God in oftentimes very subtle ways. We need to respond to that voice. We do it sometimes by emptying ourselves, making more room, dying to ourselves. Other times we do it when we fill ourselves with the events of the day. And there are other times, when we are not able to empty ourselves and not able to fill ourselves. All that we can say is: "I am sorry, Lord; be patient with me on my journey." Yet we find on this journey that we are radically changed because of what we are experiencing.

Mary experienced the unfolding of God's plan in her daily living. And she responded not only to the little daily events but also to the special ones and to the surprises. There was the death of Joseph, the call of Jesus, the reaction of the people of her own town to her Son, the event in the town synagogue, the letting go of her religious outlook and plans, and so much more. She experienced what it meant to let go of the controls and go with the flow of the Spirit.

We see the same thing happening to Peter. Besides the everyday circumstances of his life, there was a lot of the unpredictable: his call, the miraculous catch of fish, his selection as "rock," his denial of Jesus. Call to mind once again that scene in John. We hear Jesus tell Peter: "You know, when you were younger and you did what you wanted to do, you felt free, but now as you get older you will be led into places you do not want to go" (see John 21:18). There were surprises for Peter as there were surprises for Mary. The Lord has surprises for all of us. He is a God of surprises.

This brings us to the third element on this journey of fidelity.

What this commitment is going to demand of us lies beyond our personal control — and our ability to predict what is going to happen. All the vicissitudes of human nature, graced by a gracious God but still human and weak, mark our daily journey. We are *to be faithful no matter what surprises come upon us* in the midst of all of

205

this. There are days when we are able to think the best of a given situation, and other days when we are overwhelmed by our misunderstanding of the situation. There are days when our hearts are filled with childlike love and other days when our hearts feel quite cold. There are days when our emotions help us; we have a day filled with a lot of fruitful activity — a lot gets accomplished; and there are other days when just getting one thing done seems to be an insurmountable task. There are days when our imagination causes us to dance with joy because we are so loved by the Lord, and there are other days when our imagination makes us appear not as lovable as we would like to be. There are days when our memories bring back to us all the good times that we've had in our priesthood, and there are other days when it's hard to recall any good — we are overwhelmed at the particular moment with all that has gone wrong.

There are, indeed, ups and downs in living out our commitment to fidelity. We will never be able to have everything under our personal control and we will never be able to predict all that is going to happen to us. There will be surprises. We will be led to places that we know not of. In this regard, on our journeying in fidelity we have good company, the company of Jesus, Mary, and Peter.

Mary had to give constant attention and dedication to her role as mother. She watched her Son, Jesus, mature. Her perception of his identity changed from the time that he was a child to the time of his ascension. She could have rejected this need to change herself, like the rich young man in the Gospel. She could have isolated herself from her Son, because he was going in the direction that she, maybe, never thought possible. She walked in faith the walk of fidelity.

Listen to another faithful disciple, to Paul in his letter to the Galatians: ''I have been crucified with Christ; it is no longer I who live, but Christ who lives in me; and the life I now live in the flesh I live by faith in the Son of God, who loved me and gave himself for me'' (2:20).

Paul, on his journey, died to himself so that Christ

might come more alive to him and within him. He lived his life of faith faithfully because he was aware of the deep love that the Son of God had for him. This is the fourth element in our practice of the virtue of fidelity. Our commitment *demands constant attention and dedication*. Most especially our attention and dedication need to be directed to our motives for being committed. There are times when we might be faithful to our commitment to priesthood out of fear of being punished, not only by our God, but by those to whom we minister. There are times that we might live our commitment to the priesthood because of our hope for the reward. There are times when we live our commitment because of our dedication to obedience. And there are other times when we do what we must as priests because we're looking for social approval. More happy are those times when we do what we need to do because we realize that our people have a right to our service; when we live our commitment because we are moved by the goodness of those we serve. There are times when we are faithful in our service because we are aware that this is the mature love that God expects from us. And finally there are times that we minister to others because we truly believe in our hearts that those we serve are the Christ we love. To paraphrase Matthew 25:40, "Whatever we do for one of the least of our Lord's brethren, we do for the Lord."

And so we freely choose to respond to being chosen by Christ to be his priests. And we reaffirm our decision again and again, emptying ourselves, filling ourselves, and saying we're sorry when we are unable to do either. We realize that we are pledged to our Christ and that the ramifications of our pledge to Christ are beyond our ability to predict. We need to be ready for surprises as our commitment becomes ever more radical. We are aware that our commitment needs constant attention and dedication, most especially in the area of the motivation that lies behind our commitment. We have to enflesh our commitment so that we become the value, we become the gift.

As we move along we are called to reevaluate our

commitment, to look again and again at its meaning. This is a normal part of adult development; it is also part of the normal process of growing more like Christ. The greatest sin against fidelity is the refusal to grow, the refusal to be open to new possibilities. With the example of Mary, we wish to be faithful to the end, confident that with her help and intercession, we will persevere in the work that God has begun in each one of us at the moment of ordination.

It is good that we have spent some time reflecting on our beliefs, on our understanding of the faith and the fidelity of Mary. It is appropriate to reevaluate our personal devotion to Mary. Our devotion to Mary is based on the example of Christ and how he responded to his Mother. The daily rosary affords us an opportunity to prayerfully reflect on the different aspects of this.

There are two extremes that we need to avoid in our personal devotion: on the one hand an exaggeration of the role of Mary and on the other a narrow-mindedness in regard to her. We cannot become pure sentimentalists nor can we belittle the Marian mystery through extreme rationalizations. Either attitude would betray a poor understanding and appreciation of this beautiful gift of God that is his Mother. We want to develop a deep scriptural, theological, and liturgical devotion to her.

Recently I read an article by a Father Materi. It was entitled "Woman of Faith." The following excerpt from the article especially struck me, and it can serve as a summary conclusion to this chapter: "In looking at Mary one discovers not only the cost but also the joy of following Christ. She is the prototype, an image, of the Church, which must share in the suffering of our Lord in order to be resurrected and transformed into the Kingdom of God. And one discovers a woman who is loving, human, warm, faithful, humble, constantly relating everything to the God who made her. Well could she prophesy under the influence of the Spirit, 'Behold from henceforth all generations shall call me blessed, for he who is mighty has done great things for me and holy is his name.' "

Epilogue

In our journey to priesthood we have experienced many special moments. For many of us the most dramatic was the actual moment of our priestly ordination. There is a power in recalling moments such as that. It seems fitting to me that we end our journey reflecting on that moment.

Some special moments have a very special setting. Our ordination to the priesthood does, indeed, have its special setting. It was set in the same basic context as all that we do in faith: Christ (the supreme sacrament of our encounter with God) and the Church (the sacrament of unity drawing people together) — drawing the people together on the day of our ordination to the cathedral or to our religious house. The immediate setting was the sacrament of the Eucharistic Concelebration.

In such a powerful and meaningful setting, after our many years of preparation, there we were, standing before the bishop. Let us pause now for a moment and ask the Lord to be very present to us as we now seek to relive again that special experience.

The Gospel was read, and we heard the words "Let those who are to be ordained priests, come forward." Our names were called, one by one, and we answered: "*Adsum* — I am ready and willing." The priest designated by the bishop spoke in the name of the Church: "Most Reverend Father, holy mother Church requests you to ordain our brothers here present for the office of presbyter." The bishop inquired, "Do you know if they are worthy?" "I testify that upon inquiry among the People of God, and upon recommendation of those concerned with their training, they have been found worthy." Then the bishop publicly expressed his decision: "We rely on the help of the Lord God and our Savior, Jesus Christ, and we choose our brothers here present for the office of presbyter." At this the people gave voice to their feelings: "Thanks be to God!" How heartfelt that was for those who had walked with us, one way or another, on that long journey.

As the bishop went on we stood there in a sort of daze. We knew his instruction almost by heart; we had studied it so carefully, so it mattered little if we could not take it in at that moment. We knew the questions, too, but now it was time to respond to them publicly, expressing our willingness to undertake our duties: to be trusted partners with our bishop and superior, celebrating the mystery of Christ, ministering his word, and consecrating our life to God. "I am, with the help of God." We made our promise of obedience and respect. ". . . With the help of God."

We prostrated, and let the sea of fervent prayer roll over us, invoking all the mysteries of Christ, our holy mother Mary, and all the saints. Now we were ready. We knelt before the bishop. In an awesome silence, his two hands rested on our head. Other hands followed. And then the words of the consecratory prayer burned into our soul as the Spirit descended upon us and we took our place, unworthy though we were, in a long line of presbyters that stretched back to the Twelve Apostles and Jesus himself.

We were priests and the priestly vestments were placed upon us. Our hands were anointed and bound, and the instruments of celebration — bread and wine, cup and paten — were placed in them. With a kiss of peace we were welcomed into the fraternity of the presbyterate.

Whether for us these events took place last year or fifty years ago, the memory of them still has an energy that is important for us. It is there to support us in continuing to live in the fullness of that to which we were called and ordained on that special day.

I would like to share with you now some reflections on different moments in the ordination experience and what they have continued to say to me through the intervening years.

Presentation of the Candidates

The ordination rite began right after the Gospel, when we were called forth and expressed our willingness to be priests: "I am ready and willing." This is the normal time for a homily. At an ordination Mass the homily becomes a drama. Rather than words being sent forth trying to bring the Gospel home, men are consecrated and sent forth, sacraments of the headship of Christ, whose whole lives will be dedicated to bringing the Gospel home to the People of God. We are the "homily."

The men who respond to this call and say their *Adsum* are from many different backgrounds; they are of differing ages; they have had different life experiences; they bring differing visions. But they have this in common: each is willing to join with the Church in consecrating his life to witnessing to Christ. There is a powerful unity bringing together an immensely rich diversity. In this the Lord seems to say to us: "If I can share my one priesthood with men of such diversity, each one unique, then is it not evident that all can be a part of me, each with his own uniqueness? Diversity is no obstacle to our unity. If I so respect all, should you not do the same?"

On our ordination day, we were officially presented to the community. In the ensuing years we would be presented to the community again and again: with every change of assignment and with each new ministry. At this first presentation, the question is openly asked: "Do you know if they are worthy?" At each new presentation our worthiness will be questioned. The norms will not always be so clear. The competence of the judges and their objectivity will not be so sure. It is here where we are

211

confronted by the weaknesses and strengths of a human structure. If we do not have a deep inner sense of our worthiness by the grace and gift of Jesus Christ, we can be shattered and crushed. Our gifts and talents, vision and style, are his gifts — and they have their limitations. They may well serve better in one place than another, or so it may seem. But they are all we have. They are what God wants us to bring to the assignment, the ministry, for they are what he is going to use with us to accomplish what he wants us to accomplish in the place and among the people he is giving us to in service. We are worthy — by his grace.

That is why when the bishop announced his choice of us as colaborers he added that he did this with the help of the Lord. This is just one of the many times during the ordination that we are reminded of our complete dependence on the Lord. As the bishop depends here on the Lord in his discernment of God's will in our regards, so must we constantly depend on the Lord's help as we seek to discern the next step on the journey. The experience of the ministry through the years has certainly made me more and more aware of the need of prayer and quiet time to keep on discerning the Lord's will in my regard.

When the bishop made his announcement, he called forth the consent of the people. Today, with renewed active participation, this usually leads to thunderous applause. Most of the people present have good reason to celebrate. They have been with us through the long preparation. At this moment they are the Church, letting us know that we are accepted as their priests.

Such enthusiastic acceptance and approval unfortunately are not always present as we continue on our priestly journey, no matter how wholehearted our service. Often enough there is applause. But sometimes there is silence. And sometimes there is disapproval, expressed with varying degrees of vehemence. Sometimes we would be so happy just to hear one pair of hands clapping in the dark as we struggle along, trying to follow Christ as best we can. One day, during my first year as a priest, I heard that one of the parishioners had torn me apart. I went to the pastor, looking for some comfort. Instead, he simply smiled and said; "After thirty years of priesthood, I thank God we hear only about ten percent of what they say about us." Then we had a good laugh. I have never forgotten that word of wisdom and of life. Applause is great (and we should be sure to applaud our brother priests sincerely every chance we get), but we can continue without it if we have to.

The Instruction

The bishop began his long instruction. First, he spoke to the people, helping them to understand the significance of their consent. Then he spoke to us. He reminded us that although we remained members of the priesthood of all the faithful, we were to become priests in yet another way, entering into a deeper sharing in the work of Christ as teacher, priest, and pastor. He charged us to give this serious consideration, a call to live in great conformity to the likeness of Christ.

Recently, I had the privilege with some other priests to celebrate the Eucharist with the Holy Father in his private chapel. The responsorial psalm that day was: "You are a priest forever according to the order of Melchizedek." As we prayed that response it became very evident to me that the Holy Father was praying just as deeply as any of us in the group. No matter our role or title or position, our prayer to God the Father is to be a priest in the likeness of him who was prefigured by this towering figure from of old: our Lord, Jesus Christ.

The bishop continued his instruction. He called upon us to apply our energies to our sacred duties of instruction and sharing the word of God. We are to believe what we read, teach what we believe, and act in accord with what we teach. The true minister is the one who allows the word to minister to him so that he can truly minister to others, strengthening the Church in its mission of sanctifying the world in Christ. Central to this is our awareness of the mystery of the Eucharist and of the sacraments and a sense of being at the service of humankind. The hallmark of our service is that unfailing gladness of generous charity which looks after the concerns of Christ rather than our own. As the good shepherds we draw the flock together and unify it.

I did not know how much more I needed to know. On the intellectual level I was well trained, but there was so much more to be learned as that training was put into practice and deepened and made more actual by years of priestly ministry. There are many lessons still to be learned on my interior journey, still to be learned through the events of my life, still to be learned from the people who come in contact with me, from the society in which I live, from the institutional Church which I daily experience. Just when I think I have answered my questions concerning my own self-concept, my spiritual journey, my inner personal life, and my ministry, I find once again the questions arising. Each time the answers go deeper and deeper into my relationship with Christ as priest.

The Examination

In the examination by the bishop we were asked four questions: Were we resolved to work with the bishop as partners in ministry, caring for God's flock? Were we resolved to lead in the celebration of the mysteries of Christ faithfully and religiously? Were we resolved to exercise the ministry of the word of God with wisdom? Were we resolved to unite ourselves more closely each day with Christ the first priest, consecrating our lives to God for the good of all?

The life of the priest demands a constant return to the basics. Having solemnly affirmed our resolve we are henceforth accountable not only to ourselves but to the People of God, before whom we declare our resolve, and to our God. We need to constantly, albeit gently, evaluate our priestly lives in the light of these our declared resolutions.

Three times we declared, "I am," and then a fourth time, perhaps awed by all that we were undertaking, or maybe with something of Peter's desperate devotion, we added with conviction, "I am, with the help of God." We are back on the seashore with Peter; we are engaged in a very personal encounter with the Lord. We are committing ourselves not to mere service but to a very total discipleship, a daily growing union, a consecration of life.

The Promise of Obedience

As if to enflesh these resolves, to incarnate them in the Church, we went forward, knelt, and placed our hands within those of the bishop. Hands, soft and warm or cold and rigid, encircled ours, and we promised obedience to the authoritative Christ-figure in our lives. Living this promise of obedience is a challenge. An ecclesial reality, our relationship with authority, with Christ incarnated in that authority, is enfleshed in a relationship with a particular person. As the years pass, the person will change and our natural response to him will change. Bishops and superiors come and go; various human dynamics will enter into the relationship, even while the ecclesial reality remains.

I have found that for me to live this relationship with my bishop successfully I have to keep three values alive. To the amusement of my friends I call them my "three C's": communication, cooperation, and collaboration. We oftentimes find the second and third difficult, cooperation and collaboration, because we have not been working on the first: open, honest, and reciprocal communication. I wonder why there seems to be two levels of communication with our superiors. Privately, we priests have so much to say about the bishop, our superior, and the running of the diocese and community. And yet when we have the opportunity to communicate face-to-face with him, so many of us are afraid to speak up. How much healthier our dioceses and communities would be if there could be a deeper level of trust in communication.

It would lead to better cooperation and collaboration. I have also been compelled to realize that, as important as it is to work at these in my relations with those who hold authority over me, I also have to work at them in my relations with those over whom I find myself exercising the service of authority.

Even with my three C's fully in place, obedience remains obedience. There are times when we have to "bite the bullet." Our Master set the pace for us: *obediens usque at mortem. . . .* But we learn from him, too, as Cardinal Bernardin points out in a favorite phrase, "after the cross always comes the empty tomb."

The Litany of the Saints

We have expressed our resolutions, made our commitment. We hardly knew what we were undertaking. Perhaps it was with that knowledge that the bishop stood up and turned to the Church assembled, to all our relatives and friends, to all his fellow priests seasoned in laboring with him, and earnestly implored them: "Let us pray to God the Father all-powerful that he may shower the gifts of heaven on these servants of his. . . ."

And we fell flat on our faces, wanting to be drowned in the heavenly shower.

Many priests have shared with me their heartfelt belief that for them the most dramatic moment of their ordination ceremony was this time when they were lying facedown and the phrases of the litany flowed over them. Like baptism, a plunging into deep waters to rise to a new life. A sense of almost desperate need in the face of what we are undertaking. We need all those saints to be friends on the journey ahead: our particular patrons, the holy apostles, all those priests who have gone before — John Vianney, John Bosco, so many others. For me it most especially had something to do with my own prayer. It was saying in a way to all that I as a priest, even in the midst of the most important of ministries, would always have to be allowed to take time out for deep personal prayer. Even if the whole Church was assembled and waiting. It would be time for them to pray with me and for me. Here, right in the midst of the ordination rite, I was lying there, taking my rest in the Lord. For a moment, I could forget all the commitments to ministry and all the demands it rightly makes upon me and enter into an experience of oneness with our God. For the moment, others had to get along without us. We were gone for the moment, out of sight, only to be able to come back better prepared for what lies ahead. I never want to forget this particular lesson from my ordination.

I recall, as we were discussing our approaching ordination and preparing for all that we had to do, one of the concerns that aroused some hilarious scenarios was how we would handle this business of prostrating and rising again. Big feet are so apt to get caught in the hems of cassocks and albs. What a way to begin our long-dreamed-of priestly career, making complete fools of ourselves before the bishop and the whole Church! Priests are never supposed to do something like that! After years in the priesthood, I am sure we all can call up another litany, a litany of the many times we have done precisely that — made fools of ourselves in the midst of our ministry, even in the midst of some of the most sacred moments of it. Perhaps we have learned that an effective priest, one who is really there with the fullness of his humanity, is all too often playing the part of the fool for Christ's sake. Ordination to the priesthood unfortunately — or fortunately — does not save us from the normal ups and downs of life and even from falling flat on our faces on occasion. Little by little we learn the wonderful art of how to keep our dignity as priests of Jesus Christ without losing anything of our true humanity and taking refuge in some dehumanizing role playing.

The Laying on of Hands

We rose from our rest, and with emotions that can be expressed only by silence, we stepped forward and knelt before the bishop. He, too, had nothing to say at this awesome moment. Conscious of a succession that went back through the centuries, he laid his hands on our head. Other priestly hands followed, our friends, our fellow priests, wanting to share their priesthood with us.

There are times when actions say more than words can ever handle. These are the contemplative moments of life. How much I sense the need of such moments in my life: powerful, affirming moments that reanoint me to continue unflagging in my service.

We were touched by many hands at the moment of our ordination. As the years of priestly life have unfolded we have been touched again and again, all of these touches helping to make us the priests we are today. I once asked a group of priests on retreat to make a list of all those who had touched their lives along the way. I shall never forget their faces, the shining eyes, the tears as they shared the lists and realized how many people had been there for them, and were still there. (Maybe you would like to stop here for a bit and make your own list.)

The Consecratory Prayer

The movement stopped; everyone settled in place. The bishop, with his hands outstretched, began to pray. He "reminded" God of his divine plan: our personalities were to unfold to ever greater perfection, men were to be ordained to a priestly ministry to assist the pontiff, priests and Levites of old, disciples of the apostles in the new dispensation. Now it was time for the Father to pour out his Spirit upon us and make us priests to assist in the worldwide mission of this member of the episcopal college, charged to bring the Gospel to "the farthest parts of the earth."

As newly ordained priests we were ushered into the ranks of a body that reached back across the centuries and even now embraced the globe. We had taken our place in the history of the People of God in a special role. As the ceremony progressed, more would be said about our functions as priests, but first it is important to understand the essence of our priestly role. We are not primarily or exclusively confectors of the Holy Eucharist or administrators of the sacraments. To see ourselves as such would be to betray the reality. The Church is the sacrament of saving unity, and as priests we are ministers of that unity, that "all nations, gathered together in Christ, may become one holy people of God." Indeed, that all may become in truth a priestly people. All are called to be baptized into the priesthood of Christ. This day we were ordained to share in that priesthood of Christ the Head of the body. With the people, members of Christ the priest, we continue to form together one whole, one communion, one body of Christ here on earth. We have a new role in ministry, a new responsibility to minister.

Anointing of Our Hands

We were priests. We put on the vestiture of our new office. Friendly hands helped us. They assured us that fellow priests would be there to help us all along the way — if we are but ready and open to receiving such fraternal help.

We are called by the name "priests" because we offer sacrifice. The ordination ceremony now turned its attention to this characteristic office. We stretched out our hands and the bishop anointed them with holy oil and prayed that what he did exteriorly the Father would do interiorly, anointing us as he anointed Christ through the power of the Spirit. Only in this power of love could we be worthy to offer sacrifice and be instruments of sanctification.

How powerful is this age-old sign of anointing! How often in the Scriptures, as well as in history, do we find persons set apart in this way for a special role or mission! We became that day God's anointed ones, in a special way his priests.

The moment brought back a wonderful part of my growing up. My father liked to give us kids backrubs. He would use baby oil. After he had loosened up and warmed all the muscles of our neck, he would rub our hands vigorously with what oil remained on his. I would feel so alive, tingling with life. There was in all of this such a communication of love, such affirmation and empowerment to grow and be a fully alive person. The Father anointed Jesus his Son, as the bishop said, "through the power of the Holy Spirit," his Love, empowering Jesus to fulfill his mission of healing love through the sacrifice and the sanctification it would bring to us all. The Father, now through the hands of the bishop, like my natural father, reached out and anointed me in love. I felt much loved, affirmed, and empowered.

The Presentation of the Gifts

Into our newly anointed hands the bishop placed a paten and chalice, with bread and wine, for the celebration of the Eucharist. With these gifts in hand he challenged us to be aware, to be holy, to model ourselves on Christ, the true priest, the true sacrifice.

We need to be aware always of what we are about; to be aware of the deeper meaning not only of the Eucharist and sacraments but of the sacrament of each day, of the sacrament of the present moment. To be holy as the actions we perform — that means to be that of which we are a sign.

In seeking to be aware and open to what we are about, we are striving for holiness, striving to enter deeper into the mystery. This is a clear enough goal, and yet it is unsettling. The paschal mystery is, indeed, a mystery of dying to self in order to come alive again in a new and not-yet-experienced way of living. If the fears that arise in our hearts seem like a lack of faith, remember Jesus. There was no lack of faith in him. He knew what the Father was asking. Yet he did not find it easy. He was filled with such anguish and fear that he sweat blood. It was not easy for him and it is not easy for us. But in such dying there is ultimately found joy and fulfillment in the realization that "it is no longer I who live, but Christ who lives in me" (Galatians 2:20).

The Kiss of Peace

Lest we be held back by fear from truly living the life that we were called to, the bishop then embraced us, giving us the traditional kiss of peace, as did all the other priests present, assuring us that we will not be alone on the journey. After the completion of the Eucharist, our family and friends gathered around us and, as we blessed them, we received yet further assurance of prayerful and loving support as we faced what lay ahead. What a beautiful experience of Church, ordained and nonordained alike, gathered in support and mutual commitment! Perhaps we need to celebrate more anniversaries, renewing this, and not wait for silver or gold.

As I sit quietly in the glow of these memories and insights I seem to hear the Lord say to me: "I no longer call you servant but friend" — not servant, because a relationship with a servant remains on the acquaintance level, a superficial level, the level of service. We have been called to a deeper communion, the intimacy of deep sharing: "You know all that I have done among you."

This Friend sends his Spirit to us "to teach us all things, recalling to us all he has told us." "Receive the Holy Spirit as an Advocate within you." This Spirit is fire; she enflames our hearts with her love; she sets us afire, a fire that empowers us. She brings us into the inner love of the Three and at the same time she sends us forth with the power of their love.

Friendship has its condition — it must be mutual: "You are my friends if you do what I command you" (John 15:14). We want to surrender ourselves to the Divine Love, like Mary, like Jesus himself. "Do with me whatever you will." Here the relationship is complete. In this surrender, the anointing of priestly ordination can have its fullest effect and our ministry is empowered by the love that is beyond all loves.

In this love, in this friendship, in this ordination to ministry that we share in the Body of Christ, there is a bonding among us priests that we can never appreciate enough. A number of years ago I found in a newsletter a prayer that has become very special to me. Let us conclude our sharing by praying it together now:

A PRAYER FOR BROTHER PRIESTS

Risen Lord Jesus, you love us with all your priestly
        heart.
Hear my heartfelt prayer for my brother priests.
I pray for faithful and fervent priests,
   for unfaithful and tepid priests,
   for priests who labor at home and abroad,
   for tempted priests,
   for lonely and desolate priests,
   for young and old priests,
   for sick and dying priests,
   and for the priests in purgatory.
Merciful Heart of Jesus, remember that we are weak
        and frail humans.
Give us a deep faith,
   a bright and firm hope
   and a burning love.
I ask that in our loneliness, you comfort us,
   in our sorrow, you strengthen us,
   in our frustration, you show us that
    it is through suffering that the soul is purified.
Eternal High Priest, keep us close to your Sacred
        Heart
   and bless us abundantly
   in time and in eternity. Amen.
Mary, Mother of Priests, Model of Disciples, pray
        for us.

* * *

On that ordination day, we became "The Class of 19___." Our class picture is on the wall of our room. Through the years we have gathered for special occa-